Ottakars LOCAL HISTORY *Series*

Northallerton

Ottakars LOCAL HISTORY *Series*

Northallerton

Roger Cole

OTTAKAR'S

TEMPUS

Northallerton Grammar School was founded before 1322 and occupied this building from 1776, when it was built, to 1906.

Frontispiece: Part of a line of majestic purple beech trees planted on the Applegarth on 12 May 1937 to commemorate the Coronation of George VI.

First published 2002

Tempus Publishing Limited
The Mill, Brimscombe Port,
Stroud, Gloucestershire, GL5 2QG

British Library Cataloguing in Publication Data.
A catalogue record for this book is available from the British Library.

ISBN 0 7524 2673 7

Typesetting and origination by Tempus Publishing Limited
Printed in Great Britain by Midway Colour Print, Wiltshire

Contents

This striking obelisk can be found in the older parts of the cemetary and stands 'in affectionate memory of Jonathan Horner Esquire, for about forty-two years schoolmaster in the town and thrirty years master of the Grammar School. Born June 4 1805. Died 8 November 1888.'

Introduction

All of us at Ottakar's in Northallerton set out with great excitement on the venture that would become our local history project.

It was, though, an excitement liberally seasoned with fear. We are, after all, new boys and girls in town. Not for us the proud boast of being here for seven or seventeen or seventy years. Would it be thought that we didn't know about the relationship of the town and district to local history? Had we not heard of the Northallerton & District Local History Society or of the hugely productive courses in local history run by Jenny Allison? Above all, weren't we aware of the phenomenon that is Michael Riordan? Was there anything more to add?

Well yes, as this book testifies. The response was overwhelming. The interest and involvement from seasoned historian and new writer alike was immediate and passionate. We have finished up with a beguiling mixture of scholarship and anecdote, research and recollection which, taken together, give a new view of Northallerton and its surrounding area, from days long gone to the more recent past.

It is a true potpourri of times and styles. Here, for instance, among many other fantastic contributions, you can read Eleanor Atkinson's memoir of life in market gardening at Ainderby Steeple; Doreen Newcombe's recollection of the shops in 1940s Brompton; Wilson Taylor's thoughts on life as an evacuee from Sunderland in wartime Northallerton; Phoebe Newton's study of problems in educating the poor in the town in the nineteenth-century and Michael Sanders on Danby Wiske's moated rectory and manor house through the ages.

We want to thank everyone who helped with and supported the publication of this book – most particularly all the contributors who made it possible. In particular, we are grateful to the wonderful staff of the Northallerton Reference Library, who were kind and resourceful at all times. And a special thanks must indeed go to Michael Riordan who has encouraged our project from its inception and who has graced these pages with his own piece on the two world wars.

It has been a real pleasure to put this book together. We do hope that you the reader will be as delighted as we were to discover these new and enthralling aspects of the past of Northallerton and its district.

Roger Cole and staff at Ottakar's Northallerton
August, 2002

List of contributors

Jennifer Allison
Leslie Atkinson
Eleanor Ward Atkinson
E.J. Brooksbank
R.C. Dales
Jim Davie
H.H. Dyson
H.L. Fairburn
Christopher J. Gallagher
Clare Jobling
George H. Kelley
Doreen Newcombe

Phoebe Newton
Stephen P. Nunn
Phil Pidd
Valerie Plews
Michael H. Riordan
Michael Sanders
J.F. Sedgwick
Barabara Slater
Elsie Taylor
Wilson Taylor
Walter Teasdale
D.J. Thompson

The porch of the Porch House, built in 1584 amd host on two occasions, once in 1640 and again in 1647, to Charles I. The first time he was a guest, the second a prisoner.

1 Land and People

Coming into Northallerton on the Darlington Road – a timeless, tranquil scene.

Prologue

This is a story about change, and about how certain changes affect us all. Whether we know that these changes have taken place or not is a matter that only the individual can answer.

Indeed, some would say, 'What does it matter? It is today that is important to me'.

Well it does matter, because if we can understand what has happened in the past then perhaps we can see what the future holds. The past is fixed. We can't change it. But the future has not yet happened. So understanding the past and how changes have affected people may help us to predict the future. And if we don't like what we think may be, perhaps we can take steps to alter the outcome.

Thousands of years ago, this landscape that we all know today did not exist. Great sheets of ice covered the land and all was desolate. Nothing grew, nothing moved. Effectively, life did not exist. But what comes can go again, and slowly but surely the climate that brought about the ice sheet changed again and the thaw began.

What a tumultuous, awesome time that must have been. The moving ice scoured and carved, depositing immense amounts of debris in places, aided by the vast amount of melt water released. As the ice receded and the land began to warm, then the pioneer plants, shrubs and trees began the long slow process of recolonization of the wasteland. The animals began to return and they, in their turn, were followed by man.

Our ancestors, our forebears, set about changing our landscape. For the first time, people began to have a direct impact upon their surroundings.

It has, since those times, never stopped. Indeed, the pace of change has gathered speed. Today, in the space of one generation, we can change, we have changed and we still are changing the face of our landscape. That landscape is our history. Changes both great and small chart our comings and goings through historical time.

Nowhere has escaped man-made change and nowhere illustrates this better than our beloved Vale of York and the Yorkshire Dales.

Early settlers on our land would have known a far different scene from that which we know today. The changes that have taken place during the last century or so have been probably the most dramatic to have occurred, but we delude ourselves if we think that change is new. It isn't. There has always been change. All that is different is that the changes can be and often are swifter and more radical. Changes in the past, though sometimes far-reaching and altering for good the way in which ordinary people lived, did not generally remove the evidence of what had gone before. The footprints of the past could, and still can, be found if we look, and look in the right way.

Generations past tended to build on top of what was there before, only destroying what could not be left. Today, in so many ways, we destroy needlessly, probably unwittingly, the evidence of our ancestors' lives. Agricultural machinery today is so large and powerful that ancient boundaries and hedges are removed in order that deep ploughing can be done efficiently and economically. Building contractors dig deep foundations for their new developments and sweep away old buildings – buildings which probably have a design life and build quality far in excess of the probable life expectancy of the new development. That could, relatively speaking, be swept away again in no time at all. It is not just the building that has gone, but the past also.

Much has already gone, and with it our connections with those who have gone before. Much must, however, still remain to be discovered. We know much about the late and great of this land – of kings and queens, the high-born and the notorious, we know all we probably need to know.

Most of us don't come from such stock. We may be freeborn and fairly affluent but for our forbears it is highly likely that the story was far different. All the rights and changes we enjoy today were not always so. From the earliest settlers through to modern times, changes both great and small came about through the toil, suffering, intelligence and sheer hard work of ordinary men and women. They have left their mark upon this land of ours.

Perhaps we should cherish it a little more, for their sake and for our own, and for the sake of our children and all who follow them.

D.J. Thompson

2 Northallerton Caught in Time

The lion at the Golden Lion Hotel.

Northallerton caught in time

History can have many definitions. The purist historian may run screaming from the room when faced by storytelling or memories that are unsupported by sources and references. Yet the unbiased reader will, more often than not, enjoy the basic truth of a well-told anecdote or the familiarity of some recognizable local characteristic pinned down by a sharp recollection.

Northallerton has its golden share of proper historians. I cannot aspire to be one of them. What unfolds below is based effectively on a series of snapshots of our town over three centuries. Each was written in its time or recalls a period well known to the writer. Each, in its way, is brimming with enthusiasm for and pride in Northallerton. Each is inclined to be straightforward and honest at times when others might have indulged in evasion.

Taken together, they create a thread which leads us from the rather selectively-written town prospectus of 1792 to a recollection of Northallerton in 1840 and on to the chest-beating certainties of the official town handbook of 1927. The absolute truth of any of the statements and assertions that follow may at times be open to question – but I tend to think that the spirit is true and if the writers got it wrong, they did so for the right reasons.

1792

Here is the section on Northallerton from the Universal British Directory of Trade, Commerce and Manufacture. It is a short but trenchant document and rather inclined to be argumentative – if not with the reader, then certainly with other historians. In the very first paragraph, it takes 'the late learned antiquary' Roger Gale to task for alleging that Northallerton derives its name from King Alfred. You can almost hear the 'tut-tut' and see the rolling eyeballs as the writer swishes the idea away impatiently with, 'the etymology is too fanciful to be adopted.'

We are told that 'the place is commonly called Alvertonshire'. Its only street is half a mile long and well built.

The writer then begins to display a taste for the unusual in his search for items to impress. Suddenly, from contemplation of a main street with agreeable architecture, we are jerked towards a more austere corner of Northallerton: 'Amongst many other modern improvements in this town, (all undescribed, it has to be said) a new prison has been erected on the plan of the celebrated and humane Mr Howard'. All well and good, you may think, noting the interesting reference to that Mr Howard whose name is still associated with penal reform today. But our writer, having introduced the prison as a thing to set any visitor's pulse racing, now proceeds to damn it with faint praise: 'It is only an assistant to York Gaol and not a county one', we are told. And furthermore, 'it consists of but thirty cells and a place of correction and labour, with four very strong cells for capital offenders'.

We move on to what begins as a straightforward statement of Northallerton's parliamentary representation. Two members are sent to Westminster. But what follows is a complicated summary of what in the late eighteenth century was part of normal political life – restriction of the franchise, vote-rigging and apparently widespread electoral jiggery-pokery. We shouldn't be too shocked, looking back from our twenty-first century democratic seat of judgement. This was a very different world.

'The right of voting,' we are told, 'is annexed to the site of the greater part of the houses adjoining to and fronting the street. Few or none of the back tenements are considered as part of the burgage-tenures, or consequently entitled to vote.' In other words, if you were part of the majority of Northallerton's population who lived in the yards behind the High Street, the vote was a distant concept indeed. 'Some of these tenures,' our guide informs us, 'now subsist in the form of stables or cow-houses in which the appearance of one or more chimneys is usually preserved as a memorial of their right; others are let out to poor persons at a small annual rent, on the condition of keeping them in repair; and many are totally ruinous and uninhabited.'

If the vote was sold with the house (as invariably it was), 'it is considered £100 in the purchase'. The writer comments that the right of voting in the borough has invariably been annexed to the ancient and established burgage-tenures, never, as in some places, enlarged to the householders in general. He is of course talking about a distinction of rights among the well-off and worthy. Those 'poor persons' wouldn't figure in anyone's thoughts as likely voters for many decades to come.

And on goes the political dance. 'Previous to an election, in case an opposition is expected, the assignments, we are informed, of the several tenures, are prepared for such persons as the respective proprietors can confide in.' The candid and open description of this vote-rigging process is almost endearing. The writer now, however, appears to think a little qualification is called for, just in case his readers might think things had gone too far: 'But they are not executed unless called for,' he soothes. Then he wraps it up by really letting the cat out of the bag: 'Nor even then usually entrusted to the voter.' So to defeat the opposition, the proprietor is organizing votes which are registered under the names of people who will never actually cast them. And as if to recap: 'the right of election is in the burgage holders, which are about two hundred. The Bishop of Durham's bailiff is the returning-officer.' Among the 200 worthies are Ann Snowball, Inn Keeper; John Peekitt, Shoemaker; Toppy Dunn, Gent; Wilson Daggett, Apothecary; and James Langdale, Bookseller. Among the trades of the 200, the following are mentioned: skinner, flax-dresser, tinner, man-milliner, tea-dealer, tallow-chandler, glass-seller, breeches-maker, mercer, wheelwright, stockinger and mantua-maker.

After this series of searing revelations and despite some small pointers towards places of antiquity, the prospectus rather dwindles into a prosaic recitation of facts and events. One senses the writer losing interest, as if the prison and the voting system were the key issues and the rest has, rather tediously, to be squeezed in to make up the space. So we are told that there is a good market on Wednesdays for 'corn, cattle &c' and that four

fairs are held 'viz Feb 12, May 4, Sept 4 and October 2'.

We know from other sources that Northallerton was alive with drinking places at this time (as it has been throughout its history, of course). This guide confines itself to advising us that 'the principal Inns are the Golden Lion, kept by Mr Godfrey Hirst and the King's Head, kept by Mr William Bulmer'. The post office appears to have been open all hours, since the writer now mentions that it is 'shut only during the stay of the mail, which is about twenty minutes'.

That reference to the mail leads the writer on to his finale — all you needed to know about how to get out of Northallerton: 'The mail coach sets out from here to London every day at 5 o'clock in the afternoon and to the north at 5 o'clock in the morning. Fare to London, £3-13s-8d.' There was some choice and variation, however: 'The High Flyer Coach sets out to the south at four o'clock in the afternoon and to the north at eleven o'clock in the forenoon. Fare to London, £2-18s-0d.' Why this coach and the Princess Charlotte (also £2-18s-0d) were cheaper is not made clear, although, since the Charlotte and the most expensive ride both set off at 5 o'clock in the afternoon, it would be interesting to know which one got to London first! Perhaps it wasn't so much a question of speed as one of comfort, both in the fittings of the coaches and the quality of the inns at which they stayed en route. After a passing final reference to transport by stage-wagon to the capital (Handeys set out from Thomas Masterman's, Crawfords from Robert Simpson's), the prospectus splutters and dies.

An idiosyncratic approach, one might say. It's hard to imagine any modern guide majoring on the delights of prison accommodation and regimes – though, as we shall see, the political dimension and attendant controversy were not ignored by the author of the 1927 town handbook.

But let's leave our eighteenth-century companion where he began, expressing a sentiment as true now as it was then: '[Northallerton] is pleasantly situated in the North Riding of Yorkshire and is a very ancient town...'

1840

The passage of fifty years still leaves a link. This recollection of Northallerton right at the beginning of the Victorian era is based around an anonymous newspaper article published in 1910. The writer describes a lost world with intensity and passion, beginning with a description of the town in the coaching days – which is where we left our former guide.

The old London & Edinburgh mail coach was, according to this writer, established in 1785 and was worked by, among others, Mr W. Smith of the Black Bull Inn. It continued to run until 1841, when the railway killed it off. Interestingly, we are told that in 1800, a journey from London to Northallerton (some 223 miles) took forty-three hours and cost from £4 to £5. By 1840, when roads had been improved and the system of changing horses at various stages perfected (and perhaps, it might be said, under pressure from the imminent arrival of the railways), it had been reduced to twenty-two hours at a cost of twenty shillings.

The article was called 'A Glimpse Of Northallerton 70 Years Ago' and the copy I found in our wonderful reference library had been typed by (another) anonymous hand.

Again, there is the almost obligatory reference to 'only one long street', although there are some welcome descriptive additions. The houses were old with red tiles, there were narrow yards at each side of the street and the round shop windows with small square pains presented 'a very modest, homely appearance'. And a reminder that where South Parade and the houses towards Romanby now stood had been 'spread out in quiet green fields'.

The writer has axes to grind: 'In the middle of the street was the venerable market cross (opposite the Black Bull Inn), afterwards improperly pulled down and sold for £5 and now in a private garden.' Here, recalled fondly, are the 'unsightly' butchers' shambles and the old lockup and courthouse and place of public meetings; there the toll booth and the old stocks once used for drunkards; further south the archway and yard of Lodge's butcher's shop. But then, the knife comes out: 'There was no Town Hall to spoil the spaciousness of the street and to obstruct the view of the church'. The church, the writer notes, had then its 'plain barn-like chancel and its old slumberous pews. In place of the cemetery was a field'.

There is some intent to recall life accurately, sometimes with little mercy: 'The town was lit up miserably with the gas just introduced in 1835, prior to which there were still more miserable oil lamps.' Within the household, the general means of light was the double-wicked tallow candle. Our writer is almost shuddering at the memory. In the 'dim religious light of the candle, ghosts and goblins found a congenial atmosphere to breed in the imagination and the ghost story was in its proper element around the winter fire'. And after night came the problems of the dawn. 'Imagine the inconvenience of a time when there were no matches and of a cold winter's morning one had to fumble on with a flint and steel and strike sparks until the tinder was ignited'.

Our eighteenth-century guide was almost indifferent about the town's drinking habits, but not so this writer. He reckons that there were more pubs in 1840 than there were seventy years later, when there was a significantly increased population. In 1840 'they were homely old inns with sanded floors and long settles, where bluff hearty men – not perhaps so educated as at present – but with a

Looking out to today's High Street from Black Bull yard.

bluff hearty manhood, the outcome of more work and outside fresh air that was perhaps greater than the present, with a huge capacity in some of them to eat and drink, before which our modern capacity dwindles'. This sentence conjures up a picture of Northallerton nightlife which is positively bacchanalian and the writer goes on to add more detail. There were no time limits and the landlords grew 'fat, opulent, unctuous and gracious' on revenue provided by the 'jolly old topers...smoking their long churchwardens'.

That reference to 'bluff, hearty manhood' appears to be important enough for the writer to need to hammer it home: 'Men in those days were generally more given to hard drinking, hard swearing, hard eating, to fresh air, exercise and conviviable [*sic*] assembly in inns and less to reading and sitting quietly at home. It was almost regarded as a mark of manhood and prowess, even for a gentleman, to be a champion at the tankard and bottle and drink everybody else under the table.'

There were indeed more inns in these balmy times for the landlords. The New Inn stood on the corner ('next to Mr Rider's pork butcher's shop') opposite the Durham Ox. There was the Leopard Inn. The Harewood

The Market Cross – 'improperly pulled down and sold for £5 and now in a private garden' – back in its proper place.

'There was no Town Hall to spoil the spaciousness of the street and to obstruct the view of the church.'

Arms was then called by its proper name, the Tickle Toby Inn. In 1910, it had become Dunn's shoe shop, but in 1840 the building was the Wagon & Horses. 'Where Mr. Weighell lives now' stood the George Inn. On the site of the present Wesleyan chapel was the Pack Horse. The George & Dragon and the Drovers Inn had open doors. The Railway Inn at the north end was, before the railways came, called The Crown. The Railway Inn near the station was The Horse and Jockey.

It was a time when the horse, though not for much longer, held almost total sway. The inn yards and the streets were alive with horses, carts, wagons, post chaises and donkeys. The stables, empty for the most part in 1910, were then filled: 'What a horsey world when all conveyance was by horse and road. The influence and odour of horses was everywhere. It got into men's spirits. The horsey character was conspicuous in the host of stable boys, post boys, coachmen, guards and drivers.'

The writer did not elaborate on what was meant by a 'horsey character', or how exactly it showed itself. But where there were horses, could donkeys be far behind? A picture is recalled ('numbers still remember') of rows of twenty to thirty donkeys with three sacks of coal each, one at each side and one at the back. 'The coming and going of these kept the town in greater life'.

Now the writer begins to get really nostalgic. The farmer and his wife came to town in 'homely guise, far different from now, with the women pushing and the farmer pulling carts. There was not so much pride, people were more homely and neighbourly and mingled more together and went more into each others' houses'.

Life was simpler, it seems, with fewer luxuries. Tea was 6s per pound, flour 3s 6d per stone, 'or one guinea a boll of wheat, for the people ground their own flour or sent corn to the millers. Meat, poultry and eggs were, however, much cheaper'.

After some passing remarks about the old workhouse ('very homely...Mr Squince was the master'), the article ends abruptly. It is the jam of real life (or coloured memory) in the sandwich made by two more distanced presentations of the town. The 1792 version had a formal air, albeit it was personal and in parts quirky. We move on now to a view of Northallerton stamped with an official seal – but engaging and agreeably indiscrete in places for all that.

1927

This guide to Northallerton is clearly a work of pride – pride in the town and its people. It is written with huge confidence and at times an endearing swagger (he begins by referring to it as 'Ye ancient town of Northallerton') by 'JAS'.

For JAS (and, one guesses, for the complete membership of the Urban Council, who are listed proudly at the beginning), Northallerton is 'a place surrounded by all the charms and sporting possibilities of moorlands extending east for thirty miles to the sea coast and the beauties of Wensleydale and mountain and moorland west'. JAS refers to Northallerton as a quiet old town, dependent on agriculture. It has grown slowly compared with industrial towns, 'but it will to people of taste be all the sweeter and more attractive for residence'. Stick that in your pipe and smoke it, Barnsley and Halifax, he might be saying...

In 1927, the estimated population is given as 4985 (having 'more than doubled since 1801'), there are 1,205 inhabited houses, the total acreage of the town is 3,653 and the rateable value is £31,000.

Climate, says JAS is of a mild nature and the air is more bracing than in towns further north or south on account of the bracing winds which came straight from the west hills. His repetition of 'bracing' is of some interest. This was the period when the east coast resorts, particularly Skegness, were almost turning night to day by referring to the screaming gales which perennially beset them as 'bracing'. Whether there was a gentle attempt here to present Northallerton as an inland Skeggy, we may never know.

It is, according to JAS, one of the healthiest of districts. The death rate of Northallerton is very low and in 1918 (these words are written entirely without irony) it was 9.06 per thousand, one of the very lowest death rates in either urban or rural districts.

There now follows a hymn of praise to the Northallerton Urban Council for having provided the town with one of the best and purest water supplies and for having effected since 1891 such a revolution in the health of the town as to produce, one supposes, the admirable death rate already noted: 'The water is the purest and softest – as good for washing as rainwater. The gathering ground being from the heathery moorlands and direct from the springs, there is no risk of contamination.'

After a passing reference to sanitation ('most efficient'), JAS takes us headlong into Entertainment and Sport. The conjunction of these subjects for the 1920s visitor to Northallerton may seem to us strange, if not downright funny, but in some ways it is quite comforting to think that the great twenty-first-century gods of cinema and sport were in those times thought inferior in importance to the subject of sewage disposal.

There were at this time two cinemas in the town. One may hazard a guess as to which one JAS prefers. The Central Cinema in the main street, north of the town hall, is 'an elegant up-to-date place with an orchestra'. The Cinema-de-Luxe, by contrast, is simply 'on the back way to the station'. Travelling dramatic companies gave performances in the town hall. An excellent Amateur Operatic Society occasionally gave operas. And concerts, whist drives and dances provided plenty of entertainment.

The Applegarth. Bands still play here in the summer, but the sandpit is no more.

'In regard to sport', says JAS confidently, 'there is plenty'. For what he calls 'the national game of cricket', there is the old club. Football (clearly NOT then the national game) nevertheless gets more space, as JAS waxes lyrical about the cups given by the late Sir Geo. W. Elliott, the late Sir Fred A. Millbank, by the present MP for Richmond and by Lord Bolton for competitions ('with an intense spirit') in the Allertonshire League.

The golf course also provokes a purple passage: 'With its pure bracing (that word again) air and splendid view, the members have combined sources of inspiration and health.' Deeper purple for bowls: 'The serene game of bowls is provided on a velvety soft piece of turf brought from Osmotherley moors and surrounded by flowers and a scene of tranquillising beauty.'

In describing the town's tennis facilities, JAS perhaps becomes a little coy: 'For ladies and gentlemen who like each other's company...' he begins, before reeling off a list of courts – three of which are apparently open to the public at the Wensleydale Dairy Company.

Much is made of opportunities to hunt with the Bedale and Hurworth, the Zetland Hunt at Richmond, the Bilsdale ('on the heathery moors') and the South Durham.

There is, says JAS, 'capital low-ground shooting. For grouse, there are the great heathery moorlands extending from Osmotherley about thirty miles to the sea and westwards the extensive moorlands of Wensleydale and Coverdale and Swalesdale [*sic*]'.

Now the focus shifts to trade and employment and just for a moment something is revealed which perhaps shouldn't have been in such an august publication. JAS notes that the Northallerton Linoleum Company is the chief factory, employing some 200 people. The business was started forty-five years previously by Sir Geo. W. Elliott, MP for Northallerton when it was a parliamentary borough, 'as a means of getting votes'. Muted shades of 1792? We have no further indication as JAS goes serenely on to detail the linoleum, harness, horse cloths and motor car covers which are made, the thriving export and home trade the company does and its status as supplier to the War Office.

The handbook reels off full and impressive summaries of the activities of T. Place & Sons, whose timber yard and saw mills employed eighty men and supplied collieries, shipyards, boat builders and cotton and woollen mills; of the Northallerton Gas Company ('about 24 million feet of gas a year being consumed'); and of the Northallerton Light and Power Company, which had 220 Volts DC and a total maximum load of 75KW – which lit the town 'exceptionally well' (better in any event than gas did in 1840), using 'modern refractor reflector type lamps in all the main thoroughfares'.

It seems strange in the midst of all this that the activity on which JAS earlier wrote that the town depended – agriculture – gets only a desultory mention among these more localized industrial activities: 'Northallerton is noted for its splendid beef and mutton and there are two marts at which are sold the best cattle, sheep and pigs.'

JAS now describes a number of buildings and structures (the church, the town hall, the Porch House, the Old Guild Hall, the war memorial, the chapels and the schools), before coming to a section splendidly entitled 'LOCAL NOTANDA'. It might be fun in the year 2002 to find out when the last time anyone you know used the word 'notanda' – but in 1927 it was certainly going strong.

First up in LOCAL NOTANDA are the Applegarth Pleasure Gardens. 'Bands play there in the summer and a children's sand pit has been provided'. Next, JAS records with pride that a modern Motor Fire Engine has been acquired by the council.

It is now that the nineteenth century comes a-calling, as JAS describes the Poor Law Institution 'situated on the east side of town where 53 Guardians of the Poor of the Northallerton Union meet every fortnight and 49 Rural District Councillors meet every four weeks'. He then mentions the Children's Home. The Guardians have a 'very excellent Children's Home at the north end of town, which has accommodation for twelve people. It has not the appearance of an Institution and is really in the nature of a home'.

On to the 'very excellent' drill hall and the 'splendid' 900-yard rifle range run by the Territorial Army just outside the town.

A list of hotels, cafés and restaurants completes the guide - the Golden Lion Hotel, the County Hotel, South Parade, the Railway Hotel, Archer's Hotel, Russell's Café, Market Place and Tweedle's [sic] Café, Market Place, near the town hall.

That almost brings us to shops, of which none are mentioned in this (to use its own favourite word) splendid handbook, except one – which we will come to. But there are some advertisements – not many it's true, but those there are exude a confidence which is certainly (the other favourite word) bracing to the twenty-first-century reader:

'The Misses Kettlewell of the Market Place, Northallerton, are a High Class Baker and Confectioner. Wedding and Birthday Cakes are a speciality and "meat pies" [their inverted commas] are made to order.'

Also in the Market Place (when did it become the High Street?) was W. Green, tobacconist: 'Smoke our noted mixture', the advertisement cries. They had 'Walking Sticks and Pipes in Great Variety'. You could buy Green's Hygienic Pipes for 2s 6d each and Green's Special Virginia Cigarettes at 1s for twenty.

So how does JAS sign off his enthusiastic essay on 1927 Northallerton? Sternly, it must be said, even severely. Though he has mentioned nothing of the town's retail delights, he concludes in bold capitals as follows with a plea which would be recognized by any small-town trader today:

SHOPPING

SHOP IN YOUR OWN TOWN. DON'T BE DECEIVED BY THE DELUSIVE ECONOMIES OF THE CITY STORES. HELP YOUR TOWN'S TURNOVER AND THUS HELP TO KEEP DOWN THE RATES. THE LOCAL TRADERS KNOW YOU AND OFFER YOU THAT PERSONAL SERVICE UNOBTAINABLE ELSEWHERE. SHOP AT HOME.

Walter Teasdale

Ottakar's is where J. Walker, exclusive agents for the 1927 guide, used to be. Walker's were printers stationers, booksellers, toy and fancy goods dealers, fountain pen suppliers and ran a circulating library.

3 Population, Religion, Architecture, Education and Dirt

A brief population history of Northallerton

A useful introduction to any local history project is a demographic profile of the community or town being studied. Population change often reflects the success, or otherwise, in retaining, gaining or losing population in actual or relative terms. Economic factors have a particularly strong impact on population levels, with the growth of population in the industrial towns in the nineteenth century providing the most significant examples.

The decennial census enumerations beginning in 1801 provide excellent material in the modern period for the local historian. However, the parish registers from 1592, located in the North Yorkshire County Records Office, reveal significant changes in the levels of baptisms, burials and marriages within the town of Northallerton.

With the absence of census records prior to 1801, estimates of population levels have to be made with recourse to medieval taxation records held in the Public Record Office, or ecclesiastical sources. It is intended in this essay to attempt to plot the course of population change from the early medieval period to the present day and to examine some of the factors which influenced these changes.

These factors can be first broken down into the short-term, like harvest failure or pestilence, which were part and parcel of everyday life throughout the centuries. There were, however, longer-term influences on population growth not readily apparent to contemporaries and brought about by the flow of births, deaths and marriages that are, as Wrigley and Schofield put it, 'the visible outcomes of a complex and inter-related set of biological, social and economic processes'. (*The Population History of England 1541-1871*, CUP 1981).

It is widely accepted that Northallerton had its roots in the Saxon period prior to the Norman Conquest. For most of Northallerton's history, the fortunes of the town tended to be affected by the annual harvest more than any single influence. The harvest was the perennial subject of conversation in town and country, from the landowner to the cottager. Harvest was fundamental to working-class people, who often spent between 80% and 90% of their incomes on food and drink in the pre-industrial period.

W.G. Hoskins has estimated that out of a total of one hundred and forty harvests between 1480 and 1619, thirty-five – one in four – were failures. The first evidence of harvest failure to be reflected in Northallerton's burial registers is for the years 1596 and 1597, with the latter year's deficiency possibly due to the consumption of seed corn from the earlier harvest.

The harvest of 1596 was an acute disaster throughout much of Europe, with stories commonplace of people eating cats, dogs and even snakes. In Britain, the average price of corn was 83% above the norm. In Northallerton during the 'harvest year' beginning September 1596, sixty-three people died compared with the annual average of twenty-eight in the previous three calendar years.

Harvest failure often brings about the cancellation or postponement of marriages. In 1596 there were only nine marriages, followed by only four in 1597. The average for the previous years was in the region of ten to twelve marriages. These cancellations or postponements had consequences in terms of a reduced birth rate, with the number of baptisms falling to twenty-eight in 1598 from a typical figure of forty or more in previous years.

This domination of human life by the harvest continued in the seventeenth and eighteenth centuries and well into the nineteenth century. One of the last significant harvest failures was in 1846, contributing to an increase of over 50% in burials in 1847 recorded in the parish records. The number of marriages in that year was almost half that recorded in 1846.

An interesting feature of harvest performance in the nineteenth century was that over-abundant harvests could also often cause social distress due to the downward pressure on wages caused by low wheat prices. The *North Riding Calendar of Prisoners* reveals that the peak years of crime were associated not only with poor harvests, but with excessively rich ones.

Another short-term factor contributing to demographic crises was the onset of epidemics of disease like bubonic plague, typhus and influenza. There is no clear basis to estimate the population of Northallerton prior to the Black Death of 1348-49. In national terms, estimates of mortality resulting from the Black Death have ranged between one third and one half.

Even before 1348 there was downward pressure on population growth with several years of agrarian crisis between 1315 and 1322. Many Scottish incursions also took place after the Battle of Bannockburn in 1314. The North Riding was raided in 1316, 1318, 1319 and 1322, particularly in the populated arable lands – like the Northallerton area – close to the main routes. There was partial destruction of Northallerton in 1319 by the Scots and in 1322 the town was completely destroyed by fire.

There is negligible information about the impact of the Black Death on Northallerton. Evidence of the arrival of the disease in Northallerton comes, however, from the tithes of the parish church, which fell sharply in 1348 and then, after a period of recovery, began to decline steadily from 1370. In the last decade of the fifteenth century, pestilence brought about a situation where the water mill in Northallerton was vacant for want of a tenant.

In 1522 there was an outbreak of plague which prevented the holding of the Allertonshire Forestermote. There must have been many other instances of pestilence as there were many years of high mortality experience in York. The first evidence of plague, as well as the last, was recorded in the parish records in the years 1604 and 1605. There was significant mortality recorded with the letters 'pl' against each deceased's name to signify that the cause of death was plague. These deaths may not necessarily have been caused by bubonic plague, and those in 1604 in particular could have been due to a typhus epidemic. Nevertheless, in the two years, the total number dying in the two epidemics was 143 – possibly being in the region of 15% of the population of the town in 1600.

Looking at population levels in Northallerton between the fourteenth and sixteenth centuries, the earliest estimate is based upon the Poll Tax assessment of 1377 with a figure of 750 or thereabouts. The next reliable basis for calculating population levels is that of the Subsidy Payers returns of 1543-44. Assuming that 46% of the population were too poor to pay the tax, the total of ninety-one taxpayers should be increased to 168 householders. Then assuming a household size of 4.25, the resulting population of Northallerton is estimated at between 670 and 720. This is somewhat lower than the figure based upon the Poll Tax assessments and possibly reflects the adverse impact of plague or other diseases.

The population of the parish, based upon the Subsidy Payers returns (that is Northallerton, Romanby, Deighton and Great Worsall) has also been calculated at between 900 and 950. This estimate has received confirmation from the examination of a chantry certificate in 1548, which stated that within the parish there were 700 'houseling people' or communicants. Taking into consideration the children under ten years of age excluded from this figure, say 25% of the population, the resulting parish population is calculated around the 900 mark again.

There was a recovery in the second half of the sixteenth century. The growth of the population of the country has been estimated at one third and accordingly, the size of the town could have been in the region of 850 to 900 by the year 1600. The recovery in the size of the population of the town is shown in the parish registers, with a natural increase in the population of eighty-five in the decade ending 1600.

Underlying the frequent violent short-term impact imposed by the harvest cycle and major epidemics, there were other longer-term influences. The sixteenth century saw a rising population putting pressure on the available resources and a consequent decline in living standards. By the middle of the seventeenth century and until the mid-eighteenth century, there was a sharp reduction in the rate of population increase.

The Hearth Tax records of 1673 suggest that the population of Northallerton was probably less than 1,000. A note in the burial register in 1728 refers to a population of 1090, further confirming that that there had been negligible growth in the population since the late Elizabethan period.

From the data provided by Wrigley and Schofield, there was an increase in the age of females at first marriage. From the early seventeenth century, the proportion of people never marrying increased from 135-150 per thousand to 270 per thousand by the end of the century. Although this has not been confirmed by the examination of Northallerton's records, it is unlikely that they will differ in any major respect from the national data.

In any event, there are serious shortcomings in Northallerton's parish records during the seventeenth century. In Archbishop Herring's visitation return of 1743 for Northallerton, a population of no more than 1,100-1,150 could have existed.

However, a dramatic change was to take place – the census return of 1801 reveals a population of 2,138, with a further 40% increase up to 1831 revealing a rapid increase in the population of the town from the mid-1700s.

This increase in the population is largely attributed to the decline in the age of marriage of women, with the mean average falling from 26.5 between 1650 and 1699 to 23.4 between 1800 and 1849. In the decade ending 1810, the net natural growth (baptisms less burials) in Northallerton was 14.78, increasing to 15.39 in the decade ending 1830.

Nationally, the proportion who never married fell from 249 per thousand in 1701 to 68 per thousand in 1801. This rapid growth is widely accepted as being due to improved living standards, linked to the coming of the industrial revolution. As the nineteenth century progressed, there is increasing evidence of the migration of young people from Northallerton, clearly seeking better employment opportunities elsewhere.

In the 1861 census, in the age range 15-24, the percentage share of the town's population was 15.78%, with the national figures standing at 18.48%. The migration of younger people from Northallerton persists to this day, but interestingly, the 1860 figure suggests that they were being replaced by older people, particularly the over-60s. The percentage for the over-60s in Northallerton was 10.44%, compared with the national figure of 6.87%.

Finally, let us look at the census returns from the late nineteenth century up to 1991. Some key questions can be resolved in the processing of these figures allied to national data. Did the First World War result in a 'lost' generation? Can the post-war baby boom of 1947-48 be traced at local level? Is there a trend of those aged sixty or over replacing those in the age category 15-24?

Romanby has ceased to be a distinct community separate from Northallerton. In some instances, the parish boundary between the two communities passes through some people's back gardens. Accordingly, below are the census figures for both Northallerton (NAL) and Romanby (ROM), which have been combined to reflect more realistic population trends.

DATE	NAL	ROM	TOTAL
1881	3692	414	4106
1891	3802	421	4223
1901	4009	474	4483
1911	4806	537	5343
1921	4794	649	5443
1931	4786	841	5627
1951	6087	1486	7573
1961	6726	2059	8785
1971	8753	3920	12673
1981	9556	4292	13848
1991	9700	5350	15250

H.L. Fairburn

Haunted holy ground

In the thirteenth century, a new and vigorous religious movement came to the fore in this country. Its membership became known simply as the Friars.

Friars were very different from the existing cloistered monks of the time, such as those at Fountains or Rievaulx. They were much more mobile, truly evangelical and great supporters of the common people. They regularly looked after the welfare, both spiritual and physical, of some of the poorest beggars and outcasts, making themselves understandably popular with everyday citizens.

These humble men gave up their own wealth and position to minister to the sick and poor. Every major town quickly opened them with open arms. There were over five thousand Friars in England and Wales by the end of the century – perhaps one to every thousand inhabitants. It was commonplace to see a Dominican, a Franciscan, an Austin or a Carmelite wandering the bustling streets, readily offering help and prayers to all in need.

Northallerton was no exception and was actually home to two orders of Friar. From 1340 the Austins had a small dwelling-place and chapel where the Fleece Inn now stands. The Carmelites or 'White Friars' had a more substantial site which was spread across an area from today's Brompton Road to the High Street, including the land where the Rutson Hospital is located. As Leland puts it in his *Itinerary* of 1538, 'There was a house of freres in the est side of towne'. The place is also described as 'standing on the bank of the little brook called Sun-Beck'.

'Friarage Fields' covered the acres from Bullamoor Road to Turker Lane and as late as 1792 the outer walls of the Friary precinct were still discernible as faint foundations in the ground. By 1858 however, nothing was left except a 'modern wall' of reused stone –

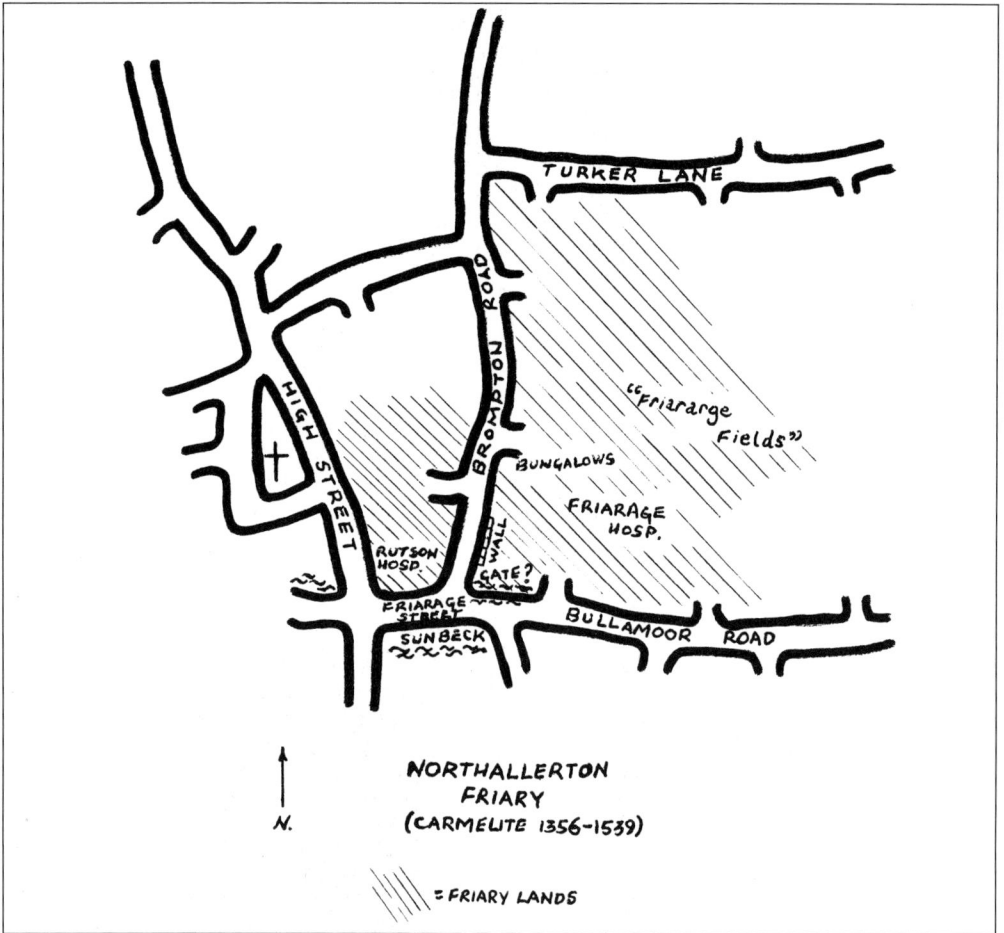

Plan of the friary lands.

doubtless the one that can still be seen in the Brompton Road today. The hospital, first established during the Second World War and later developing into the Friarage Hospital, now stands on part of the site and retains in its name a distant memory of the original religious building. Until as late as 1956, a gateway entrance to the Friary survived in the wall of what was Bell & Goldsborough's lemonade factory.

Over the centuries, human remains have also been unearthed in the locality, including six skeletons discovered during gravel extraction in 1887. Other bones were found in 1938 when some trenching work was being undertaken, and yet more in the 1960s during the construction of bungalows. These tantalizing clues begin to give us a feel for what was going on all those centuries ago. But we need to turn to documentary evidence to put flesh on those ancient bleached bones.

Records indicate that Northallerton Friary was founded in 1356 and had the distinction of being the very last Carmelite House to be established in this country. Dedicated to the Blessed Virgin Mary, it is not known for certain whether the Friary's founder/patron was Thomas Hatfield, Bishop of Durham, or

Carmelite Friar. (Drawing by Ann Puttock)

Reconstruction drawing of the cloister of Northallerton Priory. (Ann Puttock)

A wall of reused friary stone in Brompton Road

Priory Close – skeletons were discovered during the construction of bungalows during the 1960s.

Sun Beck is still located underneath the modern road system.

The Friarage Hospital stands on part of the site.

John and Helena Yole, a wealthy town merchant and his wife. We know that both helped the town's Friars in these formative years. John Yole gave them a croft called Tentour and a pasture or meadow of three acres. Edward III confirmed the foundation and Yole's land grant and actually visited the town with its new Friary the same year. Twelve months later, the Bishop of Durham granted six more acres and Lord Randolph Neville paid for the building of a complete church. This church was to be the last resting place of some very distinguished benefactors, amongst them Helena Yole, an Earl of Westmoreland and the first Prior, Walter Kellaw, who was later Provincial of the Carmelite Order and who died in 1367.

Wills and grants indicate that the Northallerton Friars enjoyed patronage from the rich and famous of the time. There were at least nineteen known benefactions, including support from Richard, Lord Scrope

of Bolton Castle (1400); Sir Thomas de Boynton of Acklam (1402); Ralph de Neville, Earl of Westmoreland (1440); and Sir Fitz-Randolph, Lord of Middleham (1457). In fact the Friars were so well thought of that in July 1502 they formed part of a reception party for Henry VII's daughter, Princess Margaret, who was on her way to marry James IV of Scotland.

Despite all their good works, the Northallerton Friary went the same way as all the other Religious Houses in the country and was dissolved on the orders of Henry VIII. The closure finally occurred on 22 December 1539 – doubtless a sad occasion for the last Prior, William Wommefraye, and his nine humble Friars, and indeed for the townspeople who had become so accustomed to their support.

Some of the Friary buildings and land passed through a succession of later owners. Richard and Henry Vavasour had the property by 1553. It was then owned by Robert Raikes Fulthorpe, then William Wailes, John Dixon, William Thrush Jefferson, Cuthbert Wilson, James O'Malley and so on.

Today, the former Friary precincts have all but disappeared under modern development, but look carefully enough and the underlying landscape can still be traced. So next time you pass the scant, stony remains in Brompton Road, spare a thought for those humble Carmelite servants of God and remember that you are passing over what can be truly described as Northallerton's 'haunted, holy ground'.

Stephen P. Nunn

Danby Wiske's moated rectory and manor house

Although its population was two-thirds that of Northallerton in the Middle Ages, Danby Wiske is now just a tiny village without shops, five miles north-west of the county capital. Apart from a church of Norman origin, its oldest structures are a surprisingly large moated site adjacent to the river Wiske and a modest manor house 200 metres away above the flood plain. An unexpected connection between the two, involving continuous occupation over the last millennium, has been suggested by recent research.

The moated site
According to English Heritage, the first structure is one of only three moated rectories in England and is thus assumed locally to have an ecclesiastical foundation. However, a combination of archaeological evidence, limited documentation and inference from what is known of similar sites elsewhere has prompted me to develop a new theory for the evolution of this intriguing scheduled site.

The inner moat is roughly square in shape, with sides about sixty yards long and six yards

wide. The full depth is about eight feet, though this is usually less than half full of water. The outer moat, which circumscribes about five acres, has been partly obliterated and no longer contains water except for one short and shallow section. Within the inner moat there is a slightly raised platform supporting the present buildings, which have evolved from an old rectory. Finney, who surveyed the whole complex for English Heritage in 1990, described this as a manorial site.

After inspecting fragments of glass and pottery recovered when the inner moat was dredged in 1996, an archaeologist reported, 'The date range of the pottery indicates that the site was in use from probably the twelfth century onwards and material was being discarded into the moat from this time, right through the medieval period and beyond. Post-medieval through to modern pottery is augmented by glass bottles from the seventeenth century to the nineteenth and confirms continuing occupation of the site'.

The first documentary evidence of occupation is the terrier of 1698, proving ecclesiastical ownership, but the 1754 presentment stated that 'The parsonage house is very much out of repair'. Indeed, successive rectors were permitted to reside elsewhere because the building was unfit to live in and in 1859, Whellan wrote, 'The Rectory House is a plain building, occupied by a labourer'. Improvements must eventually have been made as Robert Connell, who became Rector in 1883, certainly resided in the old rectory and added Glebe House as a retirement home for his parents-in-law.

The oldest part of the old rectory, now known as Moat House, is constructed of bricks characteristic of the late seventeenth century and incorporates timbers that appear to have been taken from old ships – a common building practice of that period. The complex was divided into semi-detached private

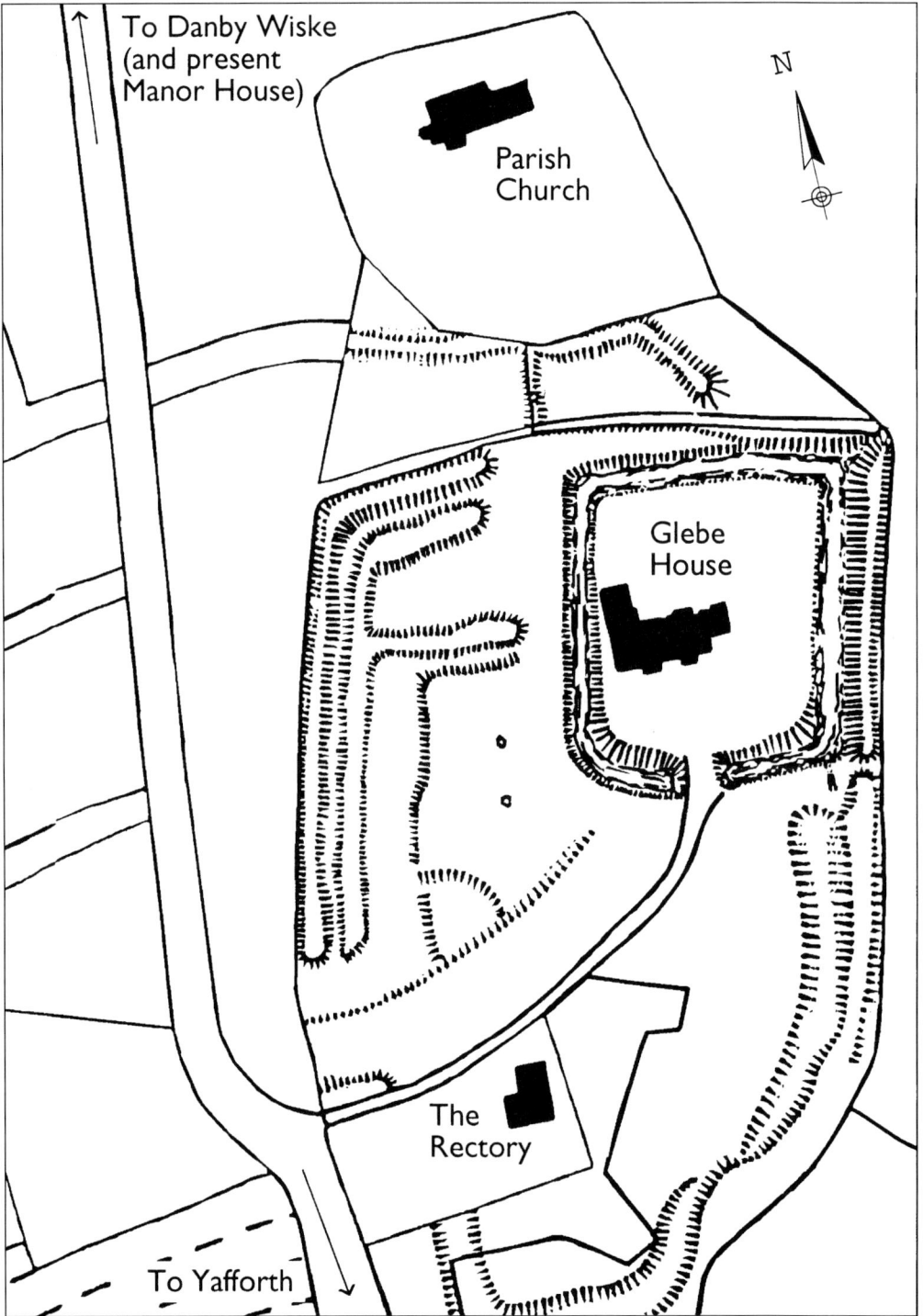

Plan of the moated site.

dwellings when sold by the church in 1962. A more modern rectory, now called Rectory House, had been built nearer the road.

Now we move into the area of informed speculation. There are 320 known examples of moated sites in Yorkshire, clustered in the lowland areas of the Vale of York and Holderness. Over half are associated with a manor house, where the church was commonly left just outside the primary enclosure as at Danby Wiske. Around 15% are associated with granges and other monastic buildings.

Many manors in the Vale of Mowbray have surviving manor house platforms surrounded by a rectangular moat. Manorial moated sites were not unknown in Anglo-Scandinavian times and it is possible that Copsi, as Earl of York under the Earl of Northumberland for most of the two decades immediately predating the Norman Conquest, used his manor of Danby Wiske as a staging post on journeys to Bamburgh and fortified it accordingly. But the double-moat configuration strongly implies a secular Norman origin, as suggested by Finney.

Like the motte at nearby Yafforth, it may have been a defensive response to the unsettled times during the civil war between Stephen and Matilda, from 1139 to 1152. This date accords with the earliest archaeological finds from the inner moat and coincides with a period when the climate was warmer and drier than it is now. However, the peak period for the construction of medieval moated buildings was 1250 to 1325, when the purpose was to enhance the status of the manorial lords. In this context, the outer moat at Danby Wiske covers a much larger area than was the norm for this region.

It is tempting to postulate that, like others in the locality, the inner moat and platform were constructed in the middle of the twelfth century by a minor local lord – in this case of the family called Mountsorrel. They sold the manor in 1236 to the more aristocratic Nevilles, who were notable fortifiers and may have dug the outer moat, enclosing five acres, in order to accommodate a large travelling retinue.

The thatched timber buildings inside the moats would not have survived the Scottish incursion of 1318, when the stone churches at both Danby Wiske and Northallerton were torched. A number of large blocks of dressed sandstone, along with charred timbers, found on the platform may represent the remains of the original manor hall. The moated site could have been reoccupied, so it may have been the deterioration in climate at that time that persuaded the incumbent lord to move his hall to the dry site of the present manor house on higher ground and grant the abandoned moated site to the church as glebe land. The original rectory, as described by Blakiston in 1698, was probably built when the higher temperatures of the fifteenth century allowed the site to be inhabited again.

Danby Wiske manor house

The present manor house is situated on a rise above the flood plain of the Wiske about 200 metres north-west of the church and the moated site – yet it was standard Norman practice to locate manor hall and church adjacent to each other. A detailed study by the Yorkshire Vernacular Buildings Study Group has provided very approximate dates for a complicated structural history.

The oldest part of the present property is the thirty-inch high sandstone plinth laid on entrenched river boulders, one chain long by one rod wide, that still forms the base of the main house. Recesses in this plinth indicate that it originally supported a two-storey timber-framed hall that would have had a thatched roof. It has been suggested that the dressed sandstone came from Harmby Quarry at the same time as the church was repaired and the moated manorial site abandoned after the Scottish depredations in the early

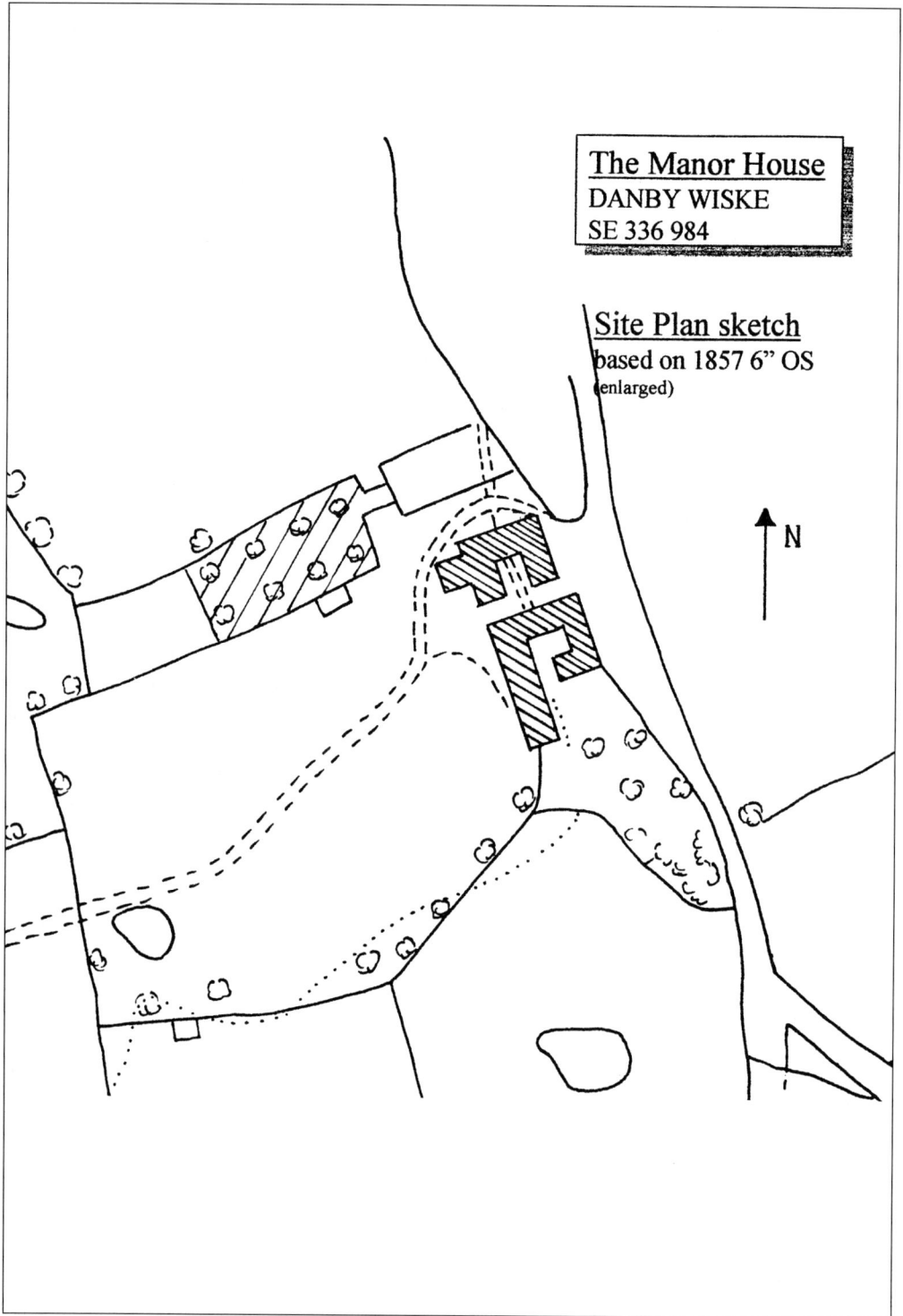

The Manor House
DANBY WISKE
SE 336 984

Site Plan sketch
based on 1857 6" OS
(enlarged)

N

The manor house – a site plan based on the 1857 Ordnance Survey.

fourteenth century. One of the Earl of Richmond's barons, Geoffrey le Scrope, held the manor at that time and could well have afforded the costs involved.

The date when the manor house was rebuilt on the stone plinth, in hand-made bricks using local clay, is more certain. Reclaimed chamfered timbers were split longitudinally and used as beams to support the first floor in the northern cell. They can still be seen in that position. A chimney stack must have been built on the north gable wall because another piece of the old timber frame, now exposed, was re-utilized as a beam across what would have been the kitchen fireplace.

The rebuilding is dated by the coat of arms above the initials T.C., displayed in a carved stone escutcheon set in the centre of the east elevation. This has been identified as that of Thomas Conyers, who was lord of the manor from 1595 to 1609. Still a Catholic sixty years after the formation of the Church of England, Thomas sold substantial farms from his manor in Danby in 1598 and 1600, probably to pay recusancy fines. Such financial pressure had the desired effect and he conformed to Anglican doctrines and paid for a named pew in the church. The rest of his family, however, continued to adhere to the old religion.

From 1609 to 1616, the manor was briefly in the hands of two other recusant gentry families. In 1616 James I granted it to his Secretary of State George Calvert (later knighted and created first Lord Baltimore), who was born locally. The grant included the mansion called the Newhall, confirming a recently constructed manor hall. Calvert's family must have been here for some time as at least one son, Philip, was born in Danby Wiske.

It seems reasonable to suggest that it was Sir George, accustomed to London fashions, who converted the manor hall into a more comfortable family house. The central hearth and stack or fire-hood were removed, the fire window and the hearth passage door blocked and a new front door installed centrally. A new stack was attached to the south gable wall, allowing the reception room to be heated. A first floor was inserted in the hall, which would previously have been open from floor to rafters. In addition, shallow-glazed windows with sills forming 'cheeks' were inserted in the upper storey to provide more light in the bedrooms. Two small windows were inserted high in the south gable to light the loft, implying that servants were snugly accommodated under the thatched roof.

Calvert built Kiplin Hall eight miles to the west four years later. He publicly reverted to Catholicism in 1625 and spent the last seven years of his life in efforts to establish a refuge in colonial America. Legal costs incurred in protracted disputes over their proprietorship of the Colony of Maryland absorbed increasing amounts of the incomes of successive Lords Baltimore, and in 1718, Danby Wiske Manor was bought by Sir Hugh Smithson of Stanwick, whose family had earlier intermarried with the Calverts.

Both Sir Hugh and his grandson of the same name, who succeeded him in 1729, were noted as energetic and businesslike agricultural improvers. They drained and fenced land, built farmhouses and cottages and required tenants to employ the latest methods. The manor house at Danby Wiske may have been occupied by a junior member of the family or by a steward in the century during which it remained under the control of the Calverts. If they had not already turned it into a tenanted farmhouse, the first Sir Hugh would have done so.

The northern chimney was removed in order to attach a two-storey barn with a through-arch threshing floor. A ground floor beam in the barn is incised 'VIIII' rather than the modern 'IX', which came into use late in the eighteenth century. But first, the roof of the house was raised about eighteen inches

The Manor House
DANBY WISKE
SE 336 984

Site Plan sketch
based on 1913 25" OS
(building use - oral information)

Thresher

Root store

Wheel
House

Cattle

Cattle

N

Yard

Granary

2 stalls

Arch to eaves

Stable under,
grain loft above

3 stalls

Byre

Arch

Loose
boxes

Dairy

1)

WC/Coal
twin

2)

1)Manor House Farm
2) Manor Farm
(Former Manor House)

0   50m

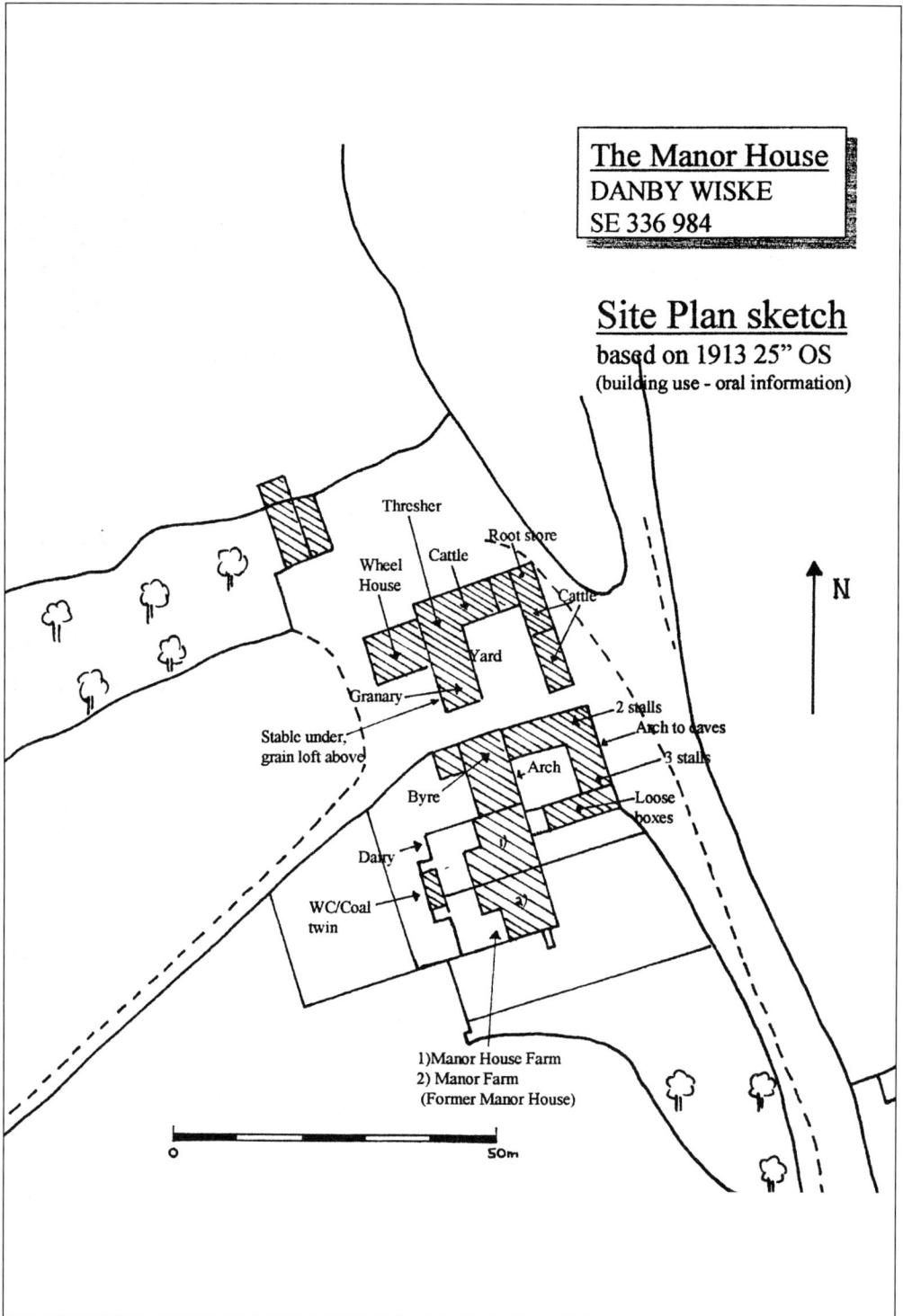

The manor house – a site plan based on the 1913 Ordnance Survey.

The old rectory.

after the installation of Yorkshire sash windows, which support the four courses of oversailing bricks above. This latter addition was continued as a design feature along the top of the new barn, integrating the external appearance of the two attached buildings to simulate the layout of a Yorkshire longhouse, the whole length being roofed with hand-made pantiles.

The loft floor of the south bay of the house was removed and a taking-in door inserted in the gable wall, with that bedroom being used for grain storage. A little later, a quadrangle of byres, with a roofed double gate allowing access from Mountstrall Lane, was added to the east of the barn – a configuration shown on a map of 1775.

The second Sir Hugh was considered to be the most handsome man of his day and, after marrying the Percy heiress and taking her noble name, was created Duke of Northumberland in 1766. In order to concentrate upon reviving the Percy fortunes, he sold some of his own properties, including the manor of Danby Wiske. This was bought by the incumbent rector, William Peacock, who had both inherited and married wealth.

With the consent of successive bishops, Peacock lived out of the parish at a house in Northallerton inherited by his wife. In 1803, however, impending legislation against absentee parsons prompted him to move into 'his own small dwelling house, nearly in the centre of his parish', which can only have been the manor house. Although sixty-eight years old, he complained that, despite having newly fitted it out, this house left his family 'so crowded and incommoded for want of rooms....that he must, of necessity, make large additions to it'.

This document neatly coincides with the modifications known to have been carried out on the manor house at about that time. The grain store in the south bay was re-converted to a bedroom by blocking up the taking-in door, installing a fireplace and adding a ceiling. The central entry was bricked in and a new door and hall created in their present positions. All the ground floor windows were replaced by Georgian sashes, one of which was also installed in the bricked-in arch when the threshing room was converted into a living room. Two access holes were punched in the apex of the north gable wall of the barn, the inside of which, at first storey level, was lined with pigeon boxes constructed of hand-made brick tiles.

William Peacock had recently inherited the adjacent Danby Hill estate on the death of his maternal grandfather – on condition that he changed his name to Cust. His eldest son and successor preferred to live at Danby Hill, so the manor house reverted to the role of a tenanted farmhouse which, in 1841, was occupied by Thomas Wilkinson with his young family and servants. To improve farming efficiency, a range of now-demolished detached farm buildings, including a wheelhouse for a threshing machine, were constructed a few metres to the north of the barn. These are shown on the Ordnance Survey map of 1857.

Both the lordship and the manor house remained in the ownership of the Custs and their trustees until 1908, when they were bought at auction by a Darlington solicitor, Thomas Clayhills, who thereby became the last known lord of the manor. Less than a year later, he sold the Danby Wiske estate to the North Riding County Council, which, prompted by the Smallholdings Act, split it into three fifty-acre tenant farms and built a

new farmhouse for the westernmost smallholding.

The other two were serviced by the old manor house, which the county council split into semi-detached farmhouses, building twin two-storey gabled extensions on the western side, adding the northern and central chimneys and inserting the square arch through the old barn. The domestic range and part of the barn were re-roofed with more regular machine-made pantiles. For the next seventy years, the two semis, then known as Manor Farm (south end) and Manor House Farm (north end), were occupied by a succession of tenant farmers.

In the 1960s, the outmoded quadrangle of small byres to the east of the barn was demolished. By 1973, the old building was becoming too expensive to maintain. The county council took advantage of the retirement of the southern occupant to build for the remaining tenant a new farmhouse (transferring to it the name Manor House Farm) and sold the longhouse for reconversion to a single private dwelling.

Michael Sanders

Obstacles to educating the poor in nineteenth-century Northallerton
Prize-winning entry

Ensuring regular attendance and keeping pupils at school long enough to acquire even basic literacy were two of the most persistent problems faced by nineteenth-century schools. Northallerton was no exception.

There was little input from the state before the first national Education Act in 1870, and up to that date, popular education was mainly promoted and financed by denominational activity. Even after legislation in 1876 which established that all children should receive elementary schooling and imposed more

The manor house.

restrictions on the employment of children, we cannot assume that education was universal. School attendance committees were not always effective, and certainly not, it appears, in our own locality, despite summonses and fines. Attendance only began to be enforced after the 1880 Education Act made it compulsory up to the age of ten. At that age a child could obtain a certificate and leave, provided he had registered enough attendances. In 1885, the National School was continuing to get, from town and country, boys of seven, eight and nine years who had not even begun their education.

Northallerton's National School often seemed to be in a state of disrepair, with frequent mentions in the logbook of broken windows. In 1876, the HMI's report described the school as dilapidated and in 'a very uncleanly state'. The master in 1884 recorded

that the closets were much in need of regular cleaning and the school floors were also dirty. He regretted the lack of a water supply on the school premises. In 1886, Dr Lumley, Medical Examiner for the Board of Health, came to inspect the school and found much to complain of. Keeping the children warm in winter could also be a problem. Each classroom had a fire, but it was an inefficient method of heating and sometimes the school was so cold that the ink froze in the inkwells! Considering the insanitary and uncomfortable conditions they endured both at home and at school, it is small wonder that children's health was often affected.

In 1849, a report had been made to the General Board of Health on living conditions in the town, where the majority of the population was crammed into overcrowded yards. There was no main drainage, most of

39

The National School in its first location at Friarage Terrace. The three houses beginning from the right-hand end were the school premises from 1810 to 1843.

the town's untreated sewage discharging itself into the Sun Beck. Privies with open soil pits were in some cases directly under sleeping rooms and poor families often kept pigs near their houses. The water supply was frequently contaminated and dwellings tended to be damp and badly ventilated.

Sometimes the Medical Officer of Health took measures to prevent the spread of infection by closing the National Schools during epidemics of scarlatina and measles. There is no doubt that they were very vulnerable to disease. In 1869, the master recorded that 'many children have died lately in the fever'. In 1878, there was another typhoid epidemic lasting for several months,

which claimed one of the school monitors among its victims. Even as late as 1895 a master was absent with typhoid and there are further mentions of the disease right up to 1900, as well as an increasing number of diphtheria cases. The infants seem to have been particularly prone to whooping cough, measles and scarlatina in the 1880s, with several deaths recorded, including a little scholar, a workhouse child, who died of whooping cough after a month's absence.

Right up to the end of the century, the National School seems to have been beset by staffing problems, with teachers leaving after a short time, being absent through illness and simply overwork. The first master to leave a record of his problems in 1864 complained of 'much disorder and want of assistance'. He seemed to have run the school single-handed for some months – no mean feat, as he commented, 'with ninety rough boys in daily attendance, it is unlikely that one person alone can conduct the school with efficiency'.

One of the main obstacles to education was absenteeism – which was not solely due to ill health. Placed in the centre of a farming area, Northallerton tended to lose many pupils to either full or part-time agricultural labour. In a British Parliamentary paper on agriculture in 1843, Mr Hugill of Northallerton was questioned about the employment of young people in the area. He was asked whether children learnt anything before going to work. He replied that boys learnt reading, writing and some arithmetic, girls reading and sewing. If they were able to earn anything, they were taken from school. Gleaning was an important activity, even to the non-agricultural families who lived in the yards. If children were not employed in hay or harvest fields, they were often keeping house for their mothers who were there. In the spring many boys were absent working in the gardens, setting potatoes.

Northallerton, as an important market town, offered many other interruptions to school life. Even on an ordinary market day, there was low attendance. In addition there were cattle, sheep, and horse fairs, agricultural shows and hirings. As late as 1890, when there was a school attendance committee in the town, the master was still complaining that 'stock market and ordinary market days are ruinous to our attendance. Quite twenty boys are engaged in driving cattle on Tuesday or in carrying messages and parcels on the market day'. Sometimes a holiday was given for a fair, but many boys stayed at home the following day as well, to clean the town and the yards afterwards.

There were far more amusements than there would have been in a small village – race meetings, elections, circuses, shooting and cricket matches, Clapton's moving diorama, Mander's Menagerie, magic lantern shows, Sanger's Waxwork Exhibition, Pepper's Ghost company and so on. Sometimes, the schoolmaster could see the educational value of certain activities, even taking the whole school to see Swallow's Circus.

The master in 1882 was less pleased when a third of his boys played truant to watch the erection of circus tents. He blamed indulgent parents for allowing their boys a half-holiday, and wrote: 'So long as this state of affairs continues, we will never be able to do the thorough work we otherwise would. The proportion of *regular attenders* is very small indeed'. In 1891, an impromptu poll by the master on one Friday's absenteeism revealed the following reasons for absence:

Minding the baby
Don't know
No boots
Expected coals, which did not come
Working with his father
Bad cough
Bad throat
Lameness (Mr Clark seemed rather sceptical about these afflictions!)
Working for Pearson the butcher
Getting cinders at the gas house
Helping mother who was cleaning upstairs
Fetching the doctor for mother
Bringing milk in the morning
Running errands in the afternoon

So many excuses seem to indicate a fairly casual attitude to schooling by many parents. A variety of measure was taken to encourage children to attend school regularly. In 1877, Kettlewell's Charity was distributed to boys for good attendance, i.e. above three hundred times a year. The master in 1882 reports that he had a 'jollification' one Friday afternoon, with races for nuts and sweets as an incentive

The National School in East Road, begun in 1842 and opened in 1843 – 'With ninety rough boys in daily attendance, it is unlikely that one person alone can conduct the school with efficiency'.

Memorial Stone on the front of the National School.

to complete the week. Later, the school was issuing printed cards for a week of full attendance. Eli Wilkinson, the attendance officer who was appointed in 1885, fairly quickly served four summonses on the parents of truanting boys and fines were imposed in two cases.

In the last decade or so of the nineteenth century, there do seem to have been some glimmerings of academic hope in Northallerton. There were opportunities where few had existed before. Some of the assistant teachers were by then trained at college in Durham and an increasing number of pupils were taking scholarships and going on to higher things, initially to the North Eastern County School at Barnard Castle and from there to university. These achievements at the end of the century seemed to mark the beginning of a more optimistic chapter in the story of local education.

Phoebe Newton

Down and dirty in Northallerton

There are plenty of pointers in the pages of history to what happened, who did what to whom, what the consequences were, who suffered, who triumphed, who endured – but not much, when it comes to it, about certain aspects of *what it was really like.*

A story is told, probably fancifully, in which a little girl approaches the mighty Doctor Johnson and with a child's lack of restraint remarks 'Oh, Doctor Johnson, how you smell!' The great lexicographer pauses, considers and turns to her in some agitation, keen to make her understand his reply. 'No, little girl,' he says, 'You smell. I stink!'

Smells. Diseases. Hygiene. Sanitation. Health. In the nineteenth century, huge waves of social reform began to break on the often filthy beaches of daily life and habits. As the

connections between sickness and dirt and between good health and cleanliness became more and more apparent, the idea took hold that hygiene and discipline were desirable ends in themselves to promote the greatest good for all the population.

Explanations of the complexities of how bodily functions were dealt with, disposed of and generally attended to are not to be found in the works of Jane Austen. One can speculate on where toilets were, how they were used, whether people brushed their teeth, how often they bathed, whether they ever washed their hair – but answers are few. We assume, from our twenty-first-century vantage point that in the general absence of soap, baths, showers, hot water, deodorants and all the other accoutrements of modern life, the odours would have been appalling. Maybe so by the refined standards of today. Perhaps to our not-so-remote ancestors, however, that was the way it was. Nasty smells and primitive waste disposal were part of life, part of its background. So, in that good old phrase, you just got on with it. It would certainly explain why in personal accounts of past times, certainly including those about Northallerton, there is precious little mention of the fouler side of daily life.

Yet it is strange that in memoirs of the early Victorian era, more was not made of the town's need for a clean break from its increasingly awful sanitary practices. It may be that the subject was not considered proper or genteel by those who wrote about Northallerton. But by 1848, a turning point had been reached with the passing of the Public Health Act. In 1849, 'we the undersigned inhabitants of the town of Northallerton in the county of York, and rated to the relief of the poor of and within that town, and being one-tenth in number of the inhabitants rated to the relief of the poor of and within the same town, do hereby petition the General Board of Health to visit the said town and to make inquiry and examination with respect thereto, with a view to the application of the said Act, according to the provisions of the said Act'.

However dense and obscure the language of this submission, there is no denying the clear plea for help it conveys. So Mr W. Ranger, Superintending Inspector of the General Board of Health, journeyed to Northallerton on 10 October 1849 and set up an enquiry in the succeeding days and months in the union boardroom. What did he find?

Mr Ranger is to the point. He tells a little of the history of the town and its current decline: 'it was, until the introduction of the railway in the district, a place of considerable thoroughfare' and takes a swipe in passing at some of the street architecture: 'at about a third of [the principal street's] length from the south end stands the tollbooth, an unsightly building and there seems no good reason for its remaining now that a new sessions-house has been erected'.

But then a glut of statistics. In 1841 there were 637 inhabited and sixty-eight uninhabited houses for a population of 3,092 people, an average of 4.24 persons to each house. In 1847, the town had spent £821 on poor relief. One in ten infants died under one year old and the average age of death was thirty-nine. Mr Ranger, in noting that the average age at death of the more healthy districts was forty-two, displays a fine Victorian grasp of the key issue – or a keen understanding of the thought patterns of the town's hard-headed leading citizens: 'The money value of the loss (of three years life) each individual can readily estimate, a circumstance in itself sufficient to show that a large economy will ensure from well-directed sanitary means of prevention.'

An analysis of number and causes of death from September 1847 to October 1849 shows that nearly one third of the total of 184 are caused by Zymotic diseases, a list including cholera, typhoid, scarlatina and smallpox. One

fifth of the deaths were classified as due to tubercular diseases.

The evidence for the need to change is now presented, and it is graphic. John Hodgson, surgeon, says: 'I have resided in the town about forty years. The privy and cesspool systems are exceedingly bad and the situation of the privies prejudicial to health as well as tending to preclude the people from acting upon principles of common decency. These privies with open soil pits are, in some cases, directly in front of the houses and in others, they are placed directly under the sleeping rooms. A privy well-placed forms the exception rather than the rule.'

J.S. Walton, surgeon and medical officer to the union, introduces a theme which recurs – a lot of it is the people's fault and the terrible conditions in which they live are incidental: 'The privy system is highly offensive; fluid excrement flows upon the surface and soaks into the ground as well as into the walls in several instances. In one instance, the occupiers of a house are even without a privy; whilst the situations where privies do exist are very objectionable. It is the practice generally with the poorer class to keep pigs near the dwellings and they continue to do so notwithstanding typhus of a malignant type has prevailed amongst them.'

The list of areas at risk is long and daunting. Mr Harrison, clerk of the union, reports that 'epidemic, endemic and contagious diseases have of late been present in George Stockwell's yard; New-row (Naisbitt's yard); Thomas Pearson's yard; Thomas Layfield's yard; Henry Pearson's yard; Rev. Mr. Green's yard or Rymer's; Black Swan yard; Ann Brown's lodging house; Anthony Carr's lodging house; James Metcalfe's dwelling house, north-end of the town; Hunter's yard; Isaac Thompson's yard; James Wheldon's yard; Mrs. Body's yard; Miss Peirse's cottages at the south end of the town; house of correction.'

Yard entrance in today's town

Why is this? A cursory look at a couple of these locations provides the answer. Hunter's yard contained twelve houses occupied by thirty-four people. The windows are placed directly over an open soil pit and pigsties. The drain for carrying off the surface foul water and other detritus passes under one of the floors and the fluid excrement flows over the surface of the yard. Of Pearson's yard, the investigation reports: 'Ingress a covered passage, 7 feet by 3 feet. Animals kept on the premises; privy pit open; pigsties close to the windows. Fever generally prevails in this yard.'

These rank conditions, widespread through all the yards and tenements, are compounded by overcrowded sleeping rooms. Mr Hodgson states that 'there is not only much overcrowding among the poorer class, but they fasten up their windows and close the fireplaces, fortifying every crevice with paper and other substitutes, avowedly to exclude the air'. Some of the reports from Mr Ranger's 'domiciliary inspection' add detail to what might otherwise appear to be an appeal for the poor to subscribe to the manly Victorian middle-class view that you can't get too much fresh air. Wilkinson's dwelling, he reports, 'comprises two rooms. A donkey and a collection of bones are kept in the back room, whilst the front room contains two beds placed foot to foot and occupied by a man, wife and five children – the eldest a son, 24; 3 girls 22, 18, 15; and 2 boys, 12 and 10 years of age'. There are numerous reports of a similar nature. Mr Walton observes that typhus fever prevails in a tenement in New yard, where five persons occupy a small room for sleeping.

The water supply is then examined. Most of it is collected from wells and many of these are polluted by sewage. Even if it is clean, however, water fetched and kept in pails is not considered safe or wholesome: 'Water retained in a sitting or other room, becoming heated and absorbing vitiated air and other impurities to the extent it dies, is rendered unfit for beverage.'

And so directly to sewage and a powerful broadside from the vicar, the Revd T. Burnett Stewart MA. Mr Burnett Stewart is much exercised by the open drain which runs from the east side of town to the west and says his piece in a letter to Mr Ranger and his committee. The drain was originally the bed of a small stream (he is of course referring to Sun Beck) and he notes that a little water still trickles along it, while once or twice a year, a torrent rushes through it and overflows its banks. But, says Mr Burnett Stewart, 'In general, especially during the summer months, its bottom consists of a filthy deposit of stinking mud and its stream consists of discoloured, offensive liquid: all who pass up and down the public streets, or cross it by the paths, perceive it. Those who live near it are the inmates of the union poorhouse. The lower part of the vicarage garden is rendered useless through the exhalation from it, which often ascends to the house and fills the rooms with its odour'.

Thomas Fowle tells Mr Ranger, 'I find the noxious gases arising from the gullyholes in the streets so very offensive that I am obliged to close the windows of my house. The sewers in their present condition are nothing more than cesspools'. And J. Whitney Smith, in describing a sewer at the south end of town with its outfall into an open ditch and then into Willow Beck, comments that 'there are 20 gully untrapped holes communicating with this sewer, a considerable portion of which is laid level, and from being constantly choked, the surface waters and sewage flow back into the yards of the houses'. Mr Whitney Smith was recalled in a memorial piece some forty years later in Smithson's *Northallerton Almanack* for 1890 as 'a neat little gentleman, who was much respected, for he took a very great interest in all that appertained to the welfare of the local community'.

Mr Ranger notes that 'after a heavy shower of rain, the inhabitants residing in the lower

Tickle Toby Yard as it is today.

Sun Beck today, alongside the Applegarth car park. Clean but not tamed.

parts of the town are for some time subjected to great annoyance'. The nature of the annoyance may in 2002 be odourless but not much else has changed, it seems, in 150 years...

The general pattern of drainage seems to be that where sewers exist, they flowed eventually into the becks – and mainly into Sun Beck. Otherwise, the foul water and sludge were habitually thrown into the beck or onto the surface.

The committee then turns its attention to the churchyard. There was concern that its location near to houses and the grammar school might create problems with burials. The churchyard was 3-5ft above the level of the road and the church floor itself was 18in-2ft 3in below the level of the churchyard. It was the sexton's habit to dig graves no deeper than 4ft. At this time, there seem to be problems with crowding. Mr W. Firbank states that the sexton 'has in no instance lately made a grave without disturbing the remains of previous burials and removed as many as five skulls in getting down a single grave. Having once commenced a grave, he digs through everything he meets with'.

The issue of whether the process of burial should be removed from the churchyard is later resolved upon Mr Ranger's recommendation. In 1849, however, Mr Burnett Stewart – while assuring the committee of his willingness to comply with its recommendations for different types of interment, or for complete removal if that is their view, nevertheless assures them that, 'I have never heard any complaint made of offensive or injurious smells proceeding at any time from any part of the churchyard'.

Mr Ranger then looks at methods of help and relief available in Northallerton for the sick. The sick-benefit clubs (the Amicable Society and the Female Benefit Club) together with the New Friendly Society were well-developed and all had comprehensive

The churchyard today, with upright gravestones removed – 'I have never heard any complaint made of offensive or injurious smells…'

and formidable sets of rules and regulations. That the advantages were open and available to a relatively restricted number of citizens (costs of membership were not cheap) cannot be denied, but the worthy intentions of the organizations and the benign principles they pursued must be applauded. It does seem that the New Friendly Society in particular was a hotbed of incident and danger. To preserve friendship and good order at their meetings, they had a complex scale of fines for bad behaviour. Among them, for cursing or swearing, the cost is 3d; for striking or attempting to use any violence to a member at any meeting, 1s; for molesting the president, treasurer, steward, or clerk in the execution of their offices, 5s; and for introducing politics, 1s.

In summarizing the state of the highways in the town, Mr Ranger notes that 'the foreman...attends to the cleansing of the streets, depositing the soil and refuse outside of the town for which a sum of 30s only is obtained. But he does not extend the process of cleansing to any of the numerous courts, passages or yards in close proximity of the houses occupied by the poorer and working classes, and where heaps of manure and refuse abound'.

Mr Ranger's remedies for the generally parlous state of things in Northallerton are, of course, simple. What they come down to are the removal of noxious refuse from the houses, streets, yards, courts and roads by good and efficient sewerage; the provision of an ample and constant supply of pure water for domestic and for general cleansing; and the keeping of the highways in good repair and order.

He writes at great length about the technical requirements involved and worries about the relative hardness of the water (13,000 cubic feet per day) if piped from various sources: 'Hard water curdles soap, and to the same extent destroys its cleansing properties and the poor, as a consequence, are left to the scanty and irregular supplies furnished by rain, which are insufficient for constant use.' Ahead of a proper survey, he favours Harrowgate Farm as a source of soft, pure and wholesome water, likely to be acceptably free, with the help of filtration, from animal, vegetable or mineral matter.

He advises that, after checking of the levels has taken place, two lines of main sewers will suffice for the discharge of the sewage and that tubular pipes need not exceed 15in in diameter. 'The effect obtainable by an efficient drainage and sewerage is no longer a question of doubt, its benefits extending even to rural districts similar to the one under consideration.'

More specifically, Mr Ranger is anxious about the drainage of the yard houses and the need to provide water closets: 'It is of the first importance that efficient means should be provided for the complete removal from the various tenements and adjacent premises of all collections of foul and decomposing matters, whether found in a liquid or a solid state. Hence the necessity for stopping all cesspools &c.' The overall cost for complete improvements he estimates at £2 5s 0d per house. One wonders whether he thought that the more reluctant worthies of the town might balk at such monies, for he adds reassuringly, 'if the work is done under the direction of the local Board and charged for by way of an improvement rate, it will only amount to about three farthings per week'.

On privies, Mr Ranger sets out his stall with some passion: 'When it is considered that closets may be constructed with a soil-pan and a siphon-trap, having all the advantages of a water closet, for a sum not exceeding £3, or if charged by way of an improvement rate, not exceeding 3s 6d per annum, there can be no just ground, as regards cost, for not giving to the poorer and working classes this addition, which is essential to their comforts, as well as to extricate them from being obliged to outrage the rules of modesty.'

There is now a rather interesting interlude in which Mr Ranger encourages the town to consider selling its liquid and solid waste for agricultural improvement – 'the value of sewage-water is no longer regarded by experienced agriculturalists as a doubtful question' – and quotes with approval Mr Smith of Deanstone who put the value of town sewage at £1 per head of the entire population. In this early advocacy of recycling, Mr Ranger is prepared to settle for less: 'The interest of the consumer must be considered, and if only a fourth of this sum be obtained, a considerable benefit will accrue to the town.' Then he makes what may be a telling point

'The churchyard is 3-5ft above the level of the road.'

about the social structure of the town and its area: 'Indeed, looking at its comparative immunity from wealthy residents or owners of lands &c, it is of the greatest consequence to the inhabitants, in a pecuniary point of view alone, that the sewage should be rendered productive.' Clearly, no noble benefactor is waiting in the wings to lend benign financial support or general patronage to the project.

In concluding, Mr Ranger is of the opinion that 'a considerable amount of sickness and consequent expense may be materially alleviated and additional comforts secured to all the inhabitants, by the application of the provisions of the Public Health Act, 1848'.

He reckons the total bill will come at most to £1,800 for public sewage and £2,300 for the water supply. Among the recommendations we have already noted, he asks in addition that all blind alleys, where practicable, be converted into thoroughfares, or 'be so opened that the noxious vapours may be dissipated by free currents of air'. He also requests ventilation of all parochial and other schools used for the children of the poor and that powers be taken to prevent overcrowding in lodging-houses and to stipulate the cubic contents of space 'for each person in the sleeping apartments of the lower-class tenements'.

One has the notion throughout that Mr Ranger is a dedicated man who knows a thing or two about getting his way. It may simply be that as a good Victorian, he has an eye for return on investment. What seems more likely is that the Northallerton people with whom he dealt are somewhat cautious about the expense involved in creating this grand new playground of healthful airs. It's pure speculation, of course, but I like to think of Mr Ranger's constant references to value for money and alternative methods of finance as subtle stages on the way to achieving his purposes.

So it is that in recommending the appointment of a twelve-person local Board of Health to take the matter in hand in the years ahead, Mr Ranger closes with a reminder typical of his quiet but constant theme. Change is needed, but it will pay dividends:

'From the best attention given to the several matters contained in this Report, I am of opinion that, by carrying out the several works as a whole, and having regard to existing charges and expenditure in labour, a positive saving may be secured to the inhabitants.'

E.J. Brooksbank

4 Lives and Living, Families and Childhood

A lifetime on the land

I am nearly seventy now, and after a lifetime working on the family farm at Hutton Bonville, my strongest memories are of things that were out of the ordinary, like seeing lightning strike a wire fence and kill chickens sheltering there. To make ends meet, many people living off the land would also engage in other work. This has been going on for so many centuries that I understand historians have a name for it: they call it the 'dual economy'.

I started young. When I was a small schoolboy, I used to catch moles, which I skinned. When the skins were dry, I sent packs of twenty at a time by post to a clothing manufacturer who paid me tenpence each for them – quite a bit of money in those days. As a result, when the primary school garden became infested with moles, the teacher, Mrs Osborne, asked me to get rid of them. I duly caught all the offending animals, but the next day I was made to write an essay about moles. What a reward!

We played the usual games at school – hopscotch, whips and tops, conkers – and the boys had a short cricket pitch in the playground. We also invented some ball games for ourselves. Those of us who lived nearby went home for dinner, but others brought sandwiches and the teacher boiled a kettle to make tea or cocoa. Miss Venetia Hildyard, whose mother had had Lovesome School built, used to come from the Hall every three months. It was like a royal visit! Other more prosaic visitors included the dentist, Mr Craven, who extracted teeth in the porch if necessary, and the 'nit nurse', Miss Brown.

Two men worked on the farm all the year round, but at busy times they were supplemented by a gang of about five Irishmen. All the workmen had supper at the farmhouse to celebrate the completion of the harvest. It was all horse work when I was a lad and we had about twelve working horses. Horse-shoeing and blacksmith work was done by a travelling blacksmith and there was a forge amongst the farm buildings. We bought our first tractor in 1939 – a Fordson 'Yellow' model on spade-lug wheels. This sounded the death-knell for horses, but none were destroyed. Dad allowed the older ones to live out their time and die naturally.

The Hildyards of Hutton Bonville Hall were very keen foxhunters and a covert on our farm always held a good number of foxes. On the days when the hunt was to take place, Dad would get up early and stop up the foxes' earths. Followers of the hunt were (or considered they were) gentry and it was not for mere farmers to associate with them. Occasionally, however, when a rider was unseated, he would give any farmer who caught his loose horse a good tip. Many famous people hunted on the land around my

Leslie Atkinson as a sixteen-year-old farm worker.

Horses bringing hay to the stacks with a paddy sweep.

farm, including Prince Charles, who had a 'good and successful day, but cold'.

A regular occurrence in the life of the farm was pig-killing day. After being killed by an expert, the pig was quickly placed in a scalding tub filled with boiling water. By rubbing or dragging a chain to and fro under its carcass, most of the hair or bristle was rubbed off. Then the pig was hoisted by its hind legs up to a beam, where it was disembowelled and the offal removed before it was cut into hams, sides etc. In the pantry, there was a bowl-shaped depression in the floor. When the pig was cut up, the sides and hams were placed meat-side down on the depression and salt rubbed into the skin.

After twenty-four hours, it was turned over and the meat side was salted and saltpetre was put down the shanks along with a little Demerera sugar. The whole lot was then covered with salt and more salt was added as necessary for three weeks – after which it was washed down and hung up to drip for a few days. When it had ceased dripping, it was hung up to dry for about three weeks before being put into bags for storage. The salt was purchased from Lewis & Cooper in solid blocks about a foot square and 2ft long. It was ground down to coarse powder by any suitable means – usually by scraping with a knife or saw. None of the animal went to waste.

We killed no other animals at the farm unless they were injured. There were no deep freezers then, so meat other than bacon would have gone off. All the fat cattle were walked to the mart in the early days, then

Loading cauliflowers onto a coop cart.

Laurie Biggins from Brompton used to take them in his cattle wagon.

We did a lot of rabbit-catching, sometimes twice a week in winter, selling them on Wednesdays to the traders who were usually waiting for us by the Market Cross in Northallerton. We also sold eggs and thirty or forty pounds of butter there, taking them by horse and trap.

More land was brought into arable use during the Second World War. Ploughing out of old grassland, some of which was really very unsuitable, was compulsory and we lost some crops altogether because the land was too wet. To improve the drainage, we employed a man for over a year to dig land drains by hand. Luckily, there was a War Agricultural Executive Committee depot at Oak Tree and we were able to hire all types of implements and tractors to help with the extra cropping.

The war also brought many evacuees, mostly from Sunderland, into the countryside. Mother was the local organizer and it was her job to distribute them around households in the area. She would collect them from the train, bring them to our farmhouse and give some of them a good wash (and in extreme cases, de-louse them) before finding them suitable billets.

Before the advent of electricity, the lamp-lit evenings were often devoted to the manufacture of clip mats, made by inserting clips, cut from worn-out clothing into hessian or sackcloth.

My brother William married the daughter of a market gardener who ran a retail shop in the old town hall in Northallerton. As a result, we started growing all types of fruit and vegetables and retailed them along with fresh eggs around the district.

We all helped William manufacture car trailers, which he sold far and wide. Even today, people still remember them. We also made poultry houses for sale, it being my job to paint the timber with creosote. On one occasion, I picked up the wrong tin and painted about a quarter of one end with black varnish before I realised my mistake. Instead of finishing the whole end with that material, I changed to the correct tin and carried on.

Leslie Atkinson's guinea pig breeding house

Gathering hives on the moors near Osmotherley.

An albino fox among early spotted orchids.

Nonetheless, a nearby farm bought that hen-house and placed it right by the roadside so that I was reminded of my error every time I went to town.

I've had several unusual enterprises over the years. For a time I bred guinea pigs for the Friarage Hospital and I also bred New Zealand white rabbits for the meat trade. They were sold at Darlington market. I also kept up to thirty-five hives of bees, moving them up to the moors in late July to produce heather honey, before I became allergic to them and had to stop. I always enjoyed ferreting rabbits and I bred a lot of ferrets for sale. A railway platelayer once came to buy a ferret and whilst making his choice, had his finger bitten. 'That's the one for me,' he said, 'I know it will bite!' My brother Norman and I laid almost all the hedges on our farm and Norman, who was also a special constable, became so skilled that he won many competitions and eventually became a judge.

I've always been very interested in wildlife and have noticed many rare and unusual things around the farm. Often, when I put down feed outdoors for sheep in winter, deer would come out of the woods to share the fodder. I saw red squirrels at play before the grey imports wiped them out. Badgers did a lot of damage among the poultry and lambs. I've seen at least two white foxes over the last ten years, but a mystery to me was a covey of ten partridges, four of which had white heads and backs with chocolate-coloured wings. I saw quite a few buzzards for a period of about three weeks not long ago and watched them fight with the local crows in the early mornings. Two large, unusual birds, which I later identified as harris hawks, were hovering one morning. They looked similar to an eagle and had a wingspan of over three feet. I have also seen a honey buzzard and a merlin.

In the season, I used to organize pheasant shoots on the farm, rearing several hundred pheasants each year. There were a large number of guests on shooting days and we always gave them an evening meal in the farmhouse. I remember that on one evening we had a power cut, which made the meal very late – but all the more enjoyable. I hatched birds using bantam hens and set some bantam eggs to increase the number of foster mothers. Unfortunately, what hatched were bantams crossed with pheasants and they were odd-looking things.

That reminds me of a near-tragedy that occurred at Hutton Bonville Hall many years ago. One of the maids had invited her boyfriend into the grounds and they were billing and cooing hidden in some bushes. The owner, Mr Hildyard, happened along with his shotgun looking to bag some game birds. Seeing some movement in the bushes, he fired in that direction. Fortunately, the only lasting damage was a loss of dignity all round!

Leslie Atkinson

Northallerton? I really do belong!

I am a southerner. Born in Kent and brought up in Devon. Coming to live in Yorkshire was a compromise between my family (in Devon) and my husband's in Newcastle!

But when we moved here in 1974, I had a letter from my Great Aunt Win, my grandfather's sister. Her mother was from Ripon, her grandmother from Northallerton – and Grannie was a Russell! This was intriguing. My mother's maiden name was Russell-Smith and she and her siblings had also been given Russell as a third Christian name. A little local research followed until we found that a Russell had built Elmcott in Hatfield Road in the 1930s, so we knocked on the door – and there they were.

Harriet Gladys Russell and Hilda Russell. Their names will be very familiar to many local people, not just because their father was

The site of Russell's café. 'The best seats were in that lovely first floor bay window.'

a well-known local bank manager, or even because they were famous in their own right as artists – but because their uncle Nathan ran Russell's café and high-class grocery store and anyone who was anybody had their coffee there. It was taken over by Hinton's, and later Safeways, but the building was what is now Superdrug and the best seats were in that lovely first-floor bay window.

Of course, I didn't know any of this yet. I was wondering how two respectable maiden ladies would react to the arrival of unknown relations!

I needn't have worried, of course. They were kindness itself and over the years became very precious to me. What is more, they revealed the most romantic family history – and were probably responsible for turning me into a local historian.

According to my new relatives, our mutual ancestor was a Nathaniel Russell, my great-great-great-grandfather, who was born in Ingleby Arncliffe and came to Northallerton from Osmotherley, possibly via Brompton as he was married there. He was a linen manufacturer whose business was eventually ruined by competition from rivals in Brompton who developed the use of water power. This is why he diversified into grocery retail.

The sisters owned a 'little red book', compiled by their grandfather or someone from an even earlier generation, tracing the family's direct male line back to a William Russell in the seventeenth century. The story in the family was that his father was lord of the manor of Old Byland. During the Civil War, Cromwell's troops had taken the father away and he was never heard of again. His wife and young son took refuge with a tenant, possibly in Hawnby. If I ever pursue family history in detail, the 'little red book' has generations of Russells listed, living in Hawnby, Osmotherley and Ingleby Arncliffe.

So how true is all this? *Baines Directory* of 1823 lists Nathaniel Russell as 'Linen

Manufacturer and Grocer'. As the former, he would have supplied spinners with flax and weavers with yarn, acting as a middle-man and part of an extensive domestic industry throughout Cleveland and North Yorkshire. After the Napoleonic Wars, the trade suffered badly from the combined effects of depression and the development of power-driven machinery, so he could well have been going into grocery at this time.

Although Northallerton certainly had a linen industry, it was on nothing like the scale of Brompton, where there were more than 200 linen weavers. The Brompton employers were powerful men and later were quick to see the importance of railways, persuading the Leeds Northern to go right through Brompton, thus securing their industry until the mid-twentieth century.

So Nathaniel lost out, but was saved by his entrepreneurial skills. His son Nathaniel was also a seed merchant – and traded in manure and guano!

One day, I hope to find out more about this earlier family history. If I can, I will be fulfilling the ambitions of my own grandfather. Gladys and Hilda remembered him visiting their father before the war and later gave me some letters he had written to Thomas Russell in the early 1920s. I had never heard of this, possibly because he was a little disappointed, having hoped to turn up a coat of arms. Also, he was a founder member of the Cromwellian Society. Perhaps that is why, in one letter, he suggests that the rebels who attacked our ancestor in Old Byland might have been part of the Pilgrimage of Grace a century earlier.

I have begun my own quest and I thought I was doing so well with Nathaniel. I think he was the first of the family to settle here as I could not find him in the list of householders for 1778, or even the 1791 *Universal British Directory*. I found him selling loads of stone to the Highways in 1812 and later serving as a member of the Select Vestry, a sign he was accepted among those of importance. Recently, I was thrilled when I thought I found him buying a big house on the High Street in the 1790s. Unfortunately, I then remembered that he was only born in 1783! This means that there must have been other Nathaniel Russells. So a lot of research now had to be done.

It certainly was my Nathaniel who joined the Northallerton Association for the Prosecution of Felons. This had been a response to the periodic disorder and high crime rate during the wars, when very high food prices caused desperation. Saywell tells, for example, of a riot here in 1804, when on Bonfire Night, the mob threw stones at General Hewgill, magistrate, of Great Smeaton. He was forced to send for a detachment of troops from Whitby. They were quartered in Northallerton for six months and thirteen of them married Northallerton women, one being the cook from the King's Head.

In 1829, as can be seen from the poster he produced under the auspices of the Association, Nathaniel was pursuing a thief. The poster reveals the dependent position of the weaver himself. He did not own the cloth he was weaving and he probably was renting the loom from Nathaniel. This was during one of the worst periods of the depression. Ten years later, there was a major Parliamentary inquiry into the plight of the hand-loom weavers and during the 1830s, many joined the Chartists. Smithson, in his Almanac of 1890, describes how in his childhood he saw bands of starving weavers coming through the town.

Nathaniel and his wife Hannah brought their family up in Northallerton. Their first child, Mary, was christened here in 1807 and after three more girls, my great-great-grandmother, Martha, was born in 1818 and the son, Nathaniel, in 1821. He was Harriet and Hilda's grandfather. I wonder if they were living in one of the yards, as Nathaniel does not show up as owner or occupier on the Tithe map of 1842. I turned to the 1841 census for help. Somewhere in the area of the present Boots, I found the family – Nathaniel and Hannah, both in their late fifties, three daughters still at home and their son. They had a fifteen-year-old servant living in.

This does not necessarily mean that they lived on the main street, as there were some substantial houses in yards – but close to them was a Russell's yard and this certainly should mean that they were in a burgage property.

Further south, still on the west side, I found another Nathaniel Russell, a plumber and glazier aged about thirty-five, with his wife and family and a fifteen-year-old servant – and a Russell's yard! Local history does tend to turn up problems rather than solve them.

The town must have been an exciting, noisy place to grow up in. Coach travel was at its busiest and there were nearly forty pubs. Many Georgian-style houses were still being built along the main street, though Standard House in 1818 shows the beginning of a change. The weekly market and huge fortnightly cattle sales were dwarfed by the massive annual fairs. The Candlemass Fair was so famous for horses that people came from the continent. It went on for a fortnight.

There was probably plenty of entertainment. Certainly concerts, plays and balls were held, many in the big room behind the King's Head, a large coaching inn on the site of the NatWest Bank.

Some of the family may well have gone to the purpose-built theatre at the end of Tickle Toby Yard, as it did not close until 1830. Among the other excitements of the next ten years were gas lighting, the celebrations for the passing of the 1832 Reform Act and for the accession of Queen Victoria.

Those living in yards would also have experienced the difficult living conditions caused by overcrowding and lack of water and

FELONY.

NORTHALLERTON
Association,
For the Prosecution of Felons, &c.

4 Guineas
REWARD

WHEREAS sometime between the Hours of **12** o'Clock last Night and **4** o'Clock this Morning, a Shop adjoining the Applegarth, in Northallerton, in the occupation of *Simon Hutton,* was feloniously entered by some Person or Persons, and **24** Yards, or thereabouts, of **LINEN CLOTH,** the Property of *Mr. Nathaniel Russell,* was cut out of a **Loom,** and feloniously stolen and carried away.

Notice is hereby Given,

That whoever will give such Information as may be the means of apprehending and convicting the Offender or Offenders, shall receive a Reward of **TWO GUINEAS** from the Committee of the said Association, and a further Reward of **TWO GUINEAS** from the said *Nathaniel Russell.*

Four guineas reward. Nathaniel Russell wasted no time in giving chase to the thieves.

Martha Judson (née Russell). She and her husband were at one time mayoress and mayor of Ripon. To Jennifer Allison's aunt Win, she was a most formidable grandmother.

Emily Smith (née Judson), 'the belle of Ripon'.

sewage. Being rather better off was no protection, particularly from disease. People were now inoculated against smallpox, but from 1830 there was the added fear of cholera, with some local places, especially Hutton Rudby, suffering very badly.

Life in Northallerton was about to see big changes. When Martha was twenty, they began to build the railway. It would open much wider horizons, but much of the bustle and drama brought by the long-distance coaches was lost. By the 1851 census, Martha had married a chemist from Ripon, Charles Judson. Her father had died but her mother, at sixty-nine, is listed in the census as 'retired grocer'. Her brother Nathaniel was now 'grocer and tea dealer' and 'head of household' but, unusually, his older sister Hannah is also described as 'grocer and tea dealer'.

I wonder if her brother continued other business interests, still in the linen trade. I found that later his son (Nathaniel!) used to transport linen from Yeoman's Mill in Brompton to Boville's Bleach Mill in Osmotherley – and he married Mary Boville. Incidentally, there is a wealth of interest in who married whom. Business married business, so the Russells became connected to the Watsons, the Tomes and the Soppets, among others.

But my branch continued in Ripon. Martha and her husband were at one time mayor and mayoress of Ripon, so there's a story I will have to follow up. To my delight, my Aunt Win remembered coming to the house in Ripon when she was a child to visit a most formidable grandmother. And there is Emily Judson, who went from Ripon to London to marry a man called Smith. She was also Aunt Win's mother, my great-grandmother – and when young, she was known as 'the Belle of Ripon'.
Another family story!

Jennifer Allison

Gardens of delight

Prize-winning entry

My father, Henry ('Harry') Robinson, was born on 27 January 1879 at Haughton-Le-Skearne, where he attended the village school. He was the eldest son of Mr and Mrs Robinson, the Market Gardeners.

In 1906 or thereabouts, he left home and, in partnership with another young man, rented the gardens and large orchard at Scruton Lane-Ends. In 1908 he married Nellie Ward of South Grange Farm and continued with the Market Gardens. With the coming of the Great War in 1914, Harry Robinson volunteered for active service and served with the Green Howards, fighting at Mons and Arras. He became a corporal and a musketry instructor. He was gassed and hospitalized but nevertheless, he fought for his country throughout the war. He was demobbed in 1918.

My mother, Nellie Robinson had continued to work the gardens during the war years. In 1921, they bought a holding in Ainderby Steeple and the business really began to grow.

I was the eldest daughter, Eleanor Ward Robinson, born 7 November, 1919.

Our schooling was at Ainderby Steeple. At school, I was taught to use a sewing machine and made outfits to wear at the annual school sports in Northallerton. Our colours were light blue and dark blue tops and shorts. For the sports day we practised down the lane as we did for drill. Annually, a group of children practised singing and then we took part in the Tournament of Song at Leyburn. We travelled by train from Ainderby station and I remember this with pleasure. Every Sunday, we cycled to Scruton to attend Sunday school and chapel and also to visit our aunts. My father was a local preacher in the Methodist church in the Bedale circuit.

My brothers and sisters and I all worked on the gardens, which had by now expanded to

Harry Robinson during the First World War.

Harry Robinson with son Ronald, friends and a very impressive motor car!

Harry recovering (back row, second right) at the Red Cross Hospital at Ickleton, Cambridgeshire, in November 1915 – 'He was gassed and hospitalized, but nevertheless fought for his country throughout the war'.

A rare aerial view of the market garden. The bales of straw with their central chimney were used to force rhubarb.

fifty acres. In 1932, my eldest brother, Ronald, had a house built on the gardens and called it Ashcroft. He married Emily Hogarth. Their son James Henry became Head Boy at Northallerton Grammar School. He was a Cuthbert scholar and also won a scholarship to London University. He taught for many years in Africa before illness brought him home. Their daughter, Alice Eleanor, is now a consultant anaesthatist.

We attended markets at Richmond and Northallerton, selling our produce. Then in 1936, my father rented a shop in the town hall at Northallerton. My job was to sell the fresh produce there. We joined the Chamber of Trade and took part in their fairs.

When the Second World War broke out, my father, because of his experience with the Army in the previous war and his knowledge of guns and firearms, was asked to form and look after a Home Guard unit at Ainderby Steeple. Quite a lot of people from the village were in the forces, although a good number were in agriculture and at least one was a Bevin boy. In wartime our workload altered. Strawberries had been our speciality. We delivered them to shops as far away as Middlesbrough and Redcar, but now we were restricted in the acreage we were allowed to grow. A boy from the village, who worked for us on the garden, was called up into the Army. He was sent to Italy and was killed on his nineteenth birthday. We also had to supply more vegetables. We supplied loads of these to the NAAFI at Catterick Garrison.

John, my youngest brother, was called up into the RAF. The girls were in the Girls Training Corps at Northallerton. We regularly had Women's Land Army girls on the gardens. It was work, work, work in those days. I opened the shop for only half the day, then worked on the land for the rest of the day.

Eleanor as a schoolgirl aged ten.

Land Army girls cutting cauliflowers ...

...and picking rhubarb.

Ronald drives the tractor; Henry tends the horse. Left to right, the Land Army girls are Ruby, 'Johnny' and Nan.

'Ten o'clock time' and a break for a photograph too. Ronald is standing, Eleanor is back row left, John is front left, Ruth is in the middle of the front row and Mary is second from right in the back row.

Commemorative photograph at Harry Robinson's official retirement at age sixty-five from the rank of Lieutenant and Platoon Commander of the Ainderby Steeple Home Guard, which he had formed and run from 1940 to 1944. Mr Robinson is in civilian clothes in the front row. The despatch rider is Butcher White from Moreton-on-Swale.

ROBINSONS (Ainderby) Ltd.

(Registered Office : Ainderby Cottage)

DIRECTORS :
MR. R. C. ROBINSON
MR. H. H. ROBINSON
MISS E. W. ROBINSON
MR. J. R. ROBINSON
MISS M. A. ROBINSON
MISS R. ROBINSON

Market Gardeners

AINDERBY

NORTHALLERTON

Yorkshire

19

The company headed notepaper. Eleanor became company secretary and learned double-entry bookkeeping.

In 1944, my father reached sixty-five and had to retire from his position with the Home Guard. He was presented by the Army officers with a silver engraved cigarette case made by Mr Clarkson, a Northallerton silversmith. Also in 1944, my father retired from gardening and a company was formed by all the members of the family. We called it Robinsons (Ainderby) Ltd.

I became a founder member of the Women's Institute. We had our committee meetings in the manor house with the black-out screens up. Petrol was rationed and coupons were required to buy clothing, sweets and food.

We remained at the town hall shop in Northallerton for over forty years until the girls married and the sons also retired. They and their wives also helped in the shop. I was voted the company secretary and attended evening classes at Northallerton Grammar School to learn double-entry bookkeeping.

In 1952, I married a farmer at Northallerton Methodist church – and that is another story.

My father died aged eighty-one years. He was ill for only about three weeks. He said, 'Old soldiers never die. They only fade away...'

Eleanor Ward Atkinson

Yards in Northallerton

The yard I lived in was called Tweddles Yard. It was named after the owner of the café and tobacconist at the top of the yard.

Like most yards, you entered by a passage about 4ft wide and 8ft high, which was usually whitewashed to make it light. Yards consisted of a row of cottages or buildings down one side facing onto the backs of the next yard. All the cottages faced south with the yards running from east to west. The width of the yards varied. The narrowest, like Barker's Yard were only about 7-8ft wide, whereas others were up to 30ft in places.

We were lucky. Our yard was about 15ft at its narrowest and faced onto one-storey outhouses, which in turn backed onto two-storey buildings in the Fleece Yard. The properties on either side of the yard in the High Street were Parker & Gardner and Hunt & Sturton Solicitors and both had living accommodation above and behind them. Attached at the back were two cottages similar in size to each other and a third cottage was set back with a lower roof, but this did have an outbuilding attached.

The first two cottages consisted of a living room about 12ft by 9ft, one bedroom and an attic. The pantry was the space created under the stairs. There was a 4ft square window at the front and back of the living room, a 3ft square window in the bedroom and a 2ft by 18in skylight in the attic.

Heating and cooking was supplied by a black-leaded open range, consisting of an oven on one side and a hob to stand a kettle or pan at the other. The fire itself was constructed with a flat shelf behind the fire grate, where fuel could be thrown and raked down when required. A coal rake was used for this purpose and this was an essential part of the fire irons as it was also used to clean the oven flues.

Water was supplied from the standpipe opposite the cottages and all the houses seemed to possess a white enamel bucket, which was filled and kept in the pantry.

Each cottage had or shared a privy, which was incorporated with an ash pit. A council workman emptied them once a week, using

his horse to pull the metal sludge cart, which had a sliding lid. By the early thirties, most of the privies had been converted to WCs, but the ash pits remained to use for refuse and ashes. The last privy I remember was converted in 1947 in Quaker Lane.

Many yards shared toilets and wash houses, but we were lucky having our own toilet and outhouse with its own set pot boiler and a cobble floor – but we did have a thirty-yard walk from the house to use the toilet. The yards that shared a washhouse had a fixed day to do the washing; so most of the yards had washing hanging out every day, except Sunday, as no one washed on a Sunday.

Light was supplied from a single gas mantle over the mantelshelf. Lamps and candles lit the rest of the house. 1930 brought electricity to Tweddles Yard and then every room was lit by electricity. Electric and gas were supplied by a penny slot meter.

At the end of the three cottages down our yard there was the British Legion Club, a

Things change and things stay the same. The Fleece carries on, but Tweddle's café has gone. The yard entrance is next to the betting shop.

A view down the modern-day entranceway.

The Royal British Legion Club, still part of the site.

two-storey building with a garden, which was walled in. This garden was later used for a single-storey extension to the club for use as a billiard room. In front of the club was a large square surrounded by three cottages. One was occupied by coal dealer T. Place. His outhouse in the square was where he kept his coal rulley and coal. The ash pit also looked onto the square.

The bottom half of the yard had a walled garth used by the council as a store yard. The house at the bottom, which faced onto East Road School, was the council cartier's and the stables were next to the store yard. Also at the bottom, next to the cartier's house, was the rear entrance to the fire station and its stores, with the front entrance being between Weldons Yard and the cartier's cottage on East Road.

The bottom half of the Fleece Yard housed the electricity board and its generators. These were powered by large steam boilers. The large round chimney at the bottom of the yard opposite the school was a prominent landmark until its removal in the 1950s.

Life in the yards could be very fickle. When everyone was agreeable, you could not wish for a better community. But when someone fell out, life could be very uncomfortable because of the closeness imposed on each family through the sharing of the toilets and the washhouses. The pride of the people who lived in the yards, in most cases, was second to none. They vied with each other for the cleanest front door step, the best donkey stoning, cleanest windows and even endeavouring to grow plants in old drainpipes and sinks to make their yard tidy and bright. The washhouse and toilets were left clean after use as either of these left dirty could cause one of the unpleasant rifts mentioned above. When a family suffered hardship through illness or death, everyone rallied round to help and in these times all arguments were forgotten.

George Kelley writes that the yard entrances were usually whitewashed to give light. Here's what they looked like when that wasn't done. By the side of the entrance to Rogerson's Yard, Mr Richard Longstaff, his daughter Jessie Longstaff (eighteen years old) and Mr Morrison pose outside their tobacconist's shop. This was taken sometime in the 1920s.

With the yards running from east to west, most of them got the evening sun. In summer most of the women would sit outside their doors after the day's work to talk, sew, knit and enjoy the evening sunshine. The children would skip or play ball near the washhouse, as this was usually the widest part of the yard. In winter, the only light in the yard was from the light through the house windows.

The yards were called after the shop at the top of the yard and this made finding the yards easy unless the shops changed hands – then it became misleading. For instance, our yard with the Tweddles nameplate was often called Parkers Yard because of the shop at the top.

The washhouses were usually a decent size. The one in Market Row was about 15ft by 12ft with the set pot boiler in one corner. Around the wall were the big iron mangles with their wooden rollers, which either belonged to a particular house or were shared by two houses. Under each mangle was a wooden or zinc-fluted tub with a dolly stick. Hanging on the walls were the zinc baths and rubbing boards. These were used for the weekly bath as well as washing the clothes. A wooden table was near the boiler for scrubbing the clothes on and this completed the equipment in the washhouse. A wooden clothes prop nearly always hung on the outside wall of each house.

The rents for the cottages varied. Ours was five shillings a week including rates. This was an average rent in the thirties.

George H. Kelley

Squatters

Northallerton is often referred to as one of the wealthiest market towns in the area. However I am sure that not a lot of the people living here now will remember that back in the late 1940s, Northallerton had its very own squatters living on what are now the outskirts of the town.

'The Hutments' were situated in the field adjacent to the Mowbray Road estate. They had been used by the soldiers during the war. Some say there were prisoners of war there, but I am too young to recall. So I will just refer to the site as belonging to the soldiers. There were four huts used for living accommodation for the men, together with a cookhouse, a chapel and a washhouse where the men could take care of their personal hygiene and wash their clothes. Halfway up the field was a sentry box, adding the final touch and, I suppose, indicating that the site was used for prisoners.

As the war came to an end, the occupants were moved out. A few families in Northallerton had their own ideas for the huts. The site took on a new use and a new meaning as several families from the town made the cookhouse and the adjoining huts their homes.

One family living in Brompton at the time heard about the site and were told to move pretty quickly if they wanted a home. There was only the chapel left. The other huts were already supporting squatters. The chapel sounded a lot better than the overcrowding they were experiencing sharing with their parents and families. The instructions from the people on the site were to move with a little furniture and then once inside to sit tight – be prepared to have the authorities try to evict but not to falter, to stay in the hut!

It was midnight when they set off from Brompton with a few pieces of furniture in a pram – a pram which the baby had just vacated. There were no streetlights to show the way and no taxis or buses to help lighten the burden – just sheer determination to have a 'home' to call their own. Once in the hut, they sat and waited. There were a few candles to light the room and keep them warm. It was a long time before people felt confident to leave the huts unattended, but everyone looked out for each other, helping to clean and paint and make the huts habitable.

These were the dwellings for the families and they prided themselves on making them their homes. Some who were clever with their hands were able to erect partitions and make bedrooms within the huts. Much later, the rural council decided to help and, I suppose, to modernize them. In so doing, the squatters became council tenants, some staying several years.

As the squatters were re-housed, 'The Hutments' were pulled down and the site was cleared. Families were dispersed to other parts of the town, where some of them still live today. All of them have happy memories of their time spent at 'The Hutments' as squatters.

Barbara Slater

A special place for a 1950s fire child

Northallerton – so many memories! It was a special place for a child of the fifties.

Home was in Linden Road, where we lived in one of the houses provided for fire brigade personnel. All the children had great times, playing round the new trees which had been planted in a square shape either side of the road in front of the houses – perfect for rounders posts. At the time, the new houses of Central Drive, the Crescent and other roads were just being built. Playing in the cul de sac was great fun and safe for the children of the area, as there was very little traffic.

Being a fireman's daughter also meant that you could be woken any time of the night, as the firemen slept at home and the alarm bells would ring in your house if they were called out. A sea of men would stream from their houses, hastily donning uniform, often over pyjamas. They would run via Dickie Harrison's farm yard (the short cut to Lascelles Lane and the former fire station, now Croft House), catch a lift with someone in the car, or get on their bikes. Once, there was a fire on the moors and the men were away for weeks; I remember the community spirit of the wives sending up meals for the men, making pack-ups to take out to them.

The best time of year for the fire children was the fire brigade Christmas party, when all the children of fire brigade-connected personnel had their annual treat. Long trestle tables were set up in the recreation hall at the fire station, accompanied by the greasy pole in the room (just in case of fire!). We ate fantastic food – I can still taste the potted meat and scrambled egg sandwiches kindly made by the fireman's wives. And the best bit – a singsong – was still to come. 'Christmas Alphabet' comes to mind, if not to tune! There were party games and the arrival of Santa Claus, who I am sure was Mr Carr.

School life started at the Applegarth at the tender age of five, where we had to have a little tin of shoe polish and a cloth to polish our desks with (if not our clothes) at the end of term. But a new building beckoned and there was a rumour that the sculpture being built in the playground of Mill Hill School at the edge of a low square wall was the start of the swimming pool that we were convinced was planned for the playground. School dinners were prepared in the kitchen there

Northallerton fire brigade Christmas party, 1955.

Mill Hill School, 1957-58.

East Road School, 1960. Mr Ramsay is in the centre of the front row.

and fruit and vegetables freshly prepared. You were teacher's pet if you were allowed to top and tail the gooseberries!

When we were older we moved on to East Road, where Mr Ramsay taught us the love of gardening at the front of the school, where each class had its own strip of garden. However, horrors lurked in the back playground in the form of air-raid shelters, which housed school equipment and produced sinister tales next to the wonderful outside toilets. The East Road location also allowed us to sneak across the road after school and paddle in the beck which ran alongside Friarage Street and Bullamoor Road. You were really brave if you paddled down the beck under the road, risking every disease promised by your friends and knowing it was strictly banned by parents!

The grammar school taught discipline and pride in the uniform, with the much-remembered Miss Webster disciplining us the next morning if we were seen outside school without full uniform, including the Panama hat.

We played long and hard and only came home for tea in the long, sunny (yes – every day!) summer holidays There used to be a cricket ground along Knotto Bottom Lane and occasionally we were allowed to help put the heavy metal numbers on the board for the scores. But that area was also our nature walk, as it was open countryside, where secrets were shared with friends and lovely wild flowers picked.

The Friarage Hospital fête was fantastic and I still have the autograph of Harry Corbett and Sooty, who opened the fête. The mile of pennies that people added to as they entered via the main gate seemed to stretch to eternity! Was the Miss Northallerton beauty contest held there also?

A special childhood in a special town – which is everything a child could hope and wish for.

Valerie Plews

Reminiscences of Mashamshire and district

I was born in 1925 at Haregill Lodge between Ellington and Ellingstring, then on the Clifton Castle estate. I have two memories of that house. It had a sunk fence between the garden and the adjoining field, which I was forbidden to climb down, although I succeeded in doing so before I left the farm as a four-year-old. The other was going into Ellingstring on a horse-drawn wagon with Mr Willie Towler, who worked for my father. We stopped at Mr Towler's garden, where he got a few hands full of green peas to eat on my way back – a habit I cannot resist to this day.

In 1929, my parents moved to a farm near Ripon, but after a very unhealthy four years returned to live at Gebdykes Farm, again on the Clifton estate. Although somewhat exposed, it gave a bird's-eye view of Masham and Lower Wensleydale to the west and the Vale of York to the east. At the end of the twentieth century, my family could celebrate seventy-five years as tenants of the Clifton Castle estate.

At Masham, I continued my education at the Church of England school, where Miss Gent was the infant teacher. Miss Steel and another were my teachers, with the headmaster Mr Young taking the senior class until the age of fourteen, which was considered school-leaving age. He also acted as church choirmaster.

On the way to school, we passed the remains of what was known as the Wooden Bridge. It once carried the light railway from Masham station to Leighton and Roundhill for the construction of the Leeds and Harrogate reservoirs, crossing the field now used for the annual traction engine rally.

We had local Sunday school outings, with sports and tea, often at a local farm. Once every two years, all the local Sunday schools joined together and went by train to Redcar.

Masham church.

The last of these excursions took place soon after the war.

One memorable event of this time was a school outing to Swinton Castle. Whether it coincided with the young Mr Cunliffe Lister's coming of age or some other event I am not sure, but we were collected from school by one of the estate's vehicles used for shooting parties. I understand that one of these vehicles is still in existence. We all returned home with a substantial present each.

An escapade of this period was a trip to the river in the dinner hour and taking a short cut to the back of the school. The area behind the present cricket pavilion was a bog, fed by the constantly running spring half way up what was known as Dixie Kell. Unfortunately, I fell into this smelly mess and was sent home, only to be reported by the bush telegraph as having drowned on my way back to school.

There was no such thing as a school dinner. We had to take a packed lunch, although we were provided with a third of a pint of milk each day. For a change we would go to Walker's fish and chip shop, where a fish cost two pence and a portion of chips one penny. To wash it down, a bottle of Theakstons lemonade could be had for one penny if you took the bottle back.

One event at this time that interfered with our education was the young Mr Cunliffe Lister landing his aeroplane on what was then known as the Showfield behind the King's Head Hotel. This happened during the dinner hour and many of us boys went to see this plane, which was quite an unusual sight in those days. This delayed our return to school and resulted in punishment being meted out by the headmaster.

Down the road in Millgate, we were able to peep through the doors of a building which housed the town's ancient manual fire pump, together with the funeral bier. The pump was removed from the town by the district council, but has recently been returned and was recently displayed at the Black Sheep Brewery.

Masham Calf Club show, 1936. Mr Dyson is on the right.

Potato pickers' tea break, 1945-46.

The standard of education was such that very few scholars passed the eleven–plus exams to go to Ripon Grammar School. After an altercation between my father and Mr Young, I was moved next door to the fee-paying grammar school that my grandfather had attended as a boarder the previous century. The fees were two shillings and sixpence a week or thirty shillings a term. As Mr Cyril Rider included both Latin and French in the curriculum, I considered this to be money well spent.

About this time in 1936, I joined the Masham Calf Club, later to become the National Federation of Young Farmers' Clubs. This meant rearing a calf for a year and keeping records of the cost of its food. The animals were subsequently entered in a show and sale. I later held the offices of treasurer and chairman of Masham YFC under the leadership of Messrs Gerald Cawthorne and Bert Verity. This and the local agricultural discussion group were the only forms of agricultural education available during the war years.

I left school a few months after my fourteenth birthday in July 1939 to work on my father's farm, then worked by horses. It was not until October 1940 that an American tractor was purchased and cultivation was mechanized.

In September 1939 war was declared on Germany and we were soon to see the children from the poor areas of Tyneside evacuated into our community. They were placed in homes with spare accommodation where they were well cared for by local people. As there were seven in our family, our house was already full.

Shortly before the war, Lord Swinton had created a new landing ground just over the river Burn by the Grewelthorpe Road, but at the outbreak of war, this was planted with concrete posts to prevent its use. Lord Swinton at this time was Air Minister and prior to the war had entertained Von Ribbentrop, the German ambassador to this country, in his shooting parties. Later in the war, I was involved in ploughing up this land for cropping by Mr Chris Jameson, the tenant.

Changes were made to the fine example of the ancient three field system known as Marfield, clearly visible from Gebdykes. The east–west plots were ploughed and cropped as part of the war effort, one by Bert Greensit, the other by Fred Caygill. Sadly, these have now been destroyed by gravel workings.

The early war years transformed the area round Masham and to the east into a giant munitions dump. This meant that all available premises were commandeered to house guards. In Masham, a company of Pioneer Corps (mainly from the south-west of England) were based to handle the large amount of munitions that came into the local stations.

I can well remember a small party of DLI regulars who came with no notice straight from Dunkirk. They took over our outbuildings, including our washhouse, which they used as a dining room. This was to guard munitions placed in the disused quarries near the farm. But 'war or not', my mother insisted they were out by 6.30 a.m. on Mondays because that was washday!

Farm labour was scarce during the war years with the need for as much home-produced food as was possible. The house known as 'The Greens' near the station was used as a hostel for Land Army girls. German and Italian prisoners of war were brought to work on farms from a camp near Thirsk.

One side effect of this period was the increased competition for local girls. Quite a few married soldiers in uniform.

One memory that lingers on from this period was of cycling home in near-pitch darkness and hearing the chorus of pheasants disturbed by distant bombing.

The main tragedy to affect the town was when a German land mine was dropped behind the White Bear Hotel, destroying three cottages and killing the four occupants of two of them, along with some soldiers billeted nearby. The occupants of the pub and one cottage escaped with their lives. It was not until fifty years later that this event was commemorated by a memorial on the site. A second mine landed on what was then the football field near Marfield House and damaged neighbouring property. Also during the war years, a Whitley bomber crashed behind Sutton Pen, and another between Masham and Snape, killing the crews.

Another tragic incident was when a young girl fell into Swinney Beck when it was in flood and was carried down the culvert to the west of the town and was drowned. A further tragedy was when a group of us from the Methodist Church were carol singing in Silver Street. Mr Young, the school headmaster, walked past us and said goodnight. That was the last time he was seen alive. He was later found drowned in the river. And around this time, a young farmer was killed when one of the first David Brown tractors in the area suffered a mechanical defect and overturned near Ilton.

The town remained famous for its annual sheep fair in September. Since the First World War they had been conducted by auction, although my father could remember sales by negotiation in the Market Place prior to 1916.

Harvest break.

The last train from Masham station.

Memorable events in wartime were the savings drives, which took on a gala atmosphere with a parade of floats depicting various aspects of the war effort. On one of these occasions, my father decided to sit on a tractor trailer surrounded by large numbers of the forms farmers were being asked to deal with. His problem was that the only driver available was his sixteen-year-old son. Not being one to openly flout the law, he merely asked the local police constable, 'Tiny' Proud (who at 6ft 8in tall was reputed to be the tallest policeman in the force), beforehand to shut an eye while I drove him round.

During the war and post-war years, a half-term holiday in October was unheard of. It was potato-picking holiday and the local schoolmaster consulted the farmers as to when the crop was ready for harvesting. The use of chemicals to hasten ripening was uncommon then. The holiday was usually in the first or second week in October. My father used to employ up to about thirty children of varying ages. They were paid accordingly and collected from and returned to Masham each day. It was interesting to hear them discussing how they were going to spend their earnings – often on Christmas presents for their families. Parents were not so generous with pocket money in those days and it let the children know the value of money.

The end of hostilities came as a relief as we looked forward to the lifting of the many restrictions that had curtailed our activities. Some, however, like food and petrol rationing, were to continue for some time. Any celebrations consisted of hastily-constructed bonfires. The fireworks were mostly surplus Home Guard shot gun cartridges fired into the air.

Major Burril returned to his home at 'The Greens' after war service, only to be irritated by the fact that his land and occasionally his house were flood by the river Ure. So in true

Mr Dyson doing voluntary work, 1999.

military style, he persuaded the local quarry owner to put a charge of gelignite under the weir across the river between his land and the disused mill on the opposite bank, to lower the flood level.

In the 1930s and 1940s there was a regular bus service between Masham and Ripon, with two buses leaving early morning, one via Tanfield and the other via Grewelthorpe. I understand use of this service declined and until recently there was no regular bus service between Masham, Bedale and Northallerton except for a weekly market-day bus service to Bedale.

In my school days, the Shaw's from Ellington went on a Tuesday by horse and trap to Bedale market. It is surprising that it has taken sixty years for a bus service to be provided, with the nearest major hospital at Northallerton making this essential.

And how could I forget the winter of early 1947. The last day the ground was not too hard to plough was the first of January. The ground remained frozen until the end of January, when heavy snowfalls began and the lying snow remained until the end of March. Fortunately, Hunters at Gebdykes Quarry had the council snowplough and most roads were kept open.

I hope these recollections of life in Masham and district prove to be of interest to those who read them and I apologise to those who deserve a mention whom I have omitted.

H.H. Dyson

Ruddy Metcalfes

All too often, entries in the assorted parish registers of the eighteenth and early nineteenth centuries from Bedale, Crakehall, Great Fencote, Snape and Well are redolent with the implied disapproval of entries such as spurious child, illegitimate child and mother wanting a husband. Even in more recent instances, such as that of Auntie Kitty's own parents, the knot was sometimes only tied a matter of weeks before a serious embarrassment occurred.

Auntie Kitty was the youngest of four siblings, all of whom were born between 1886 and 1898 to William and Catherine Metcalfe. Her father, an agricultural labourer who was a quarter of a century older than his wife, died before his daughter's second birthday, so she was brought up by her mother alone. A widow at thirty-seven, her mother fought against what might have appeared insuperable odds to haul her young family up by the bootstraps. This upbringing by a mother who was set upon a course of upward social mobility may account for Auntie Kitty having held certain misconceptions about the family antecedence.

She was a woman of some traditional rectitude and respectability, a ruddy and robust golfing spinster in later life, living on the Kent coast. If she was aware of a blanket having a 'wrong side' she certainly never entertained the possibility that her own forbears owed anything to it.

It was during one of her annual visits to my parents' home in York in the 1970s that she first revealed a curiosity about her ancestors and a determination to 'research the family history.' It was a determination coloured by a blithe assumption that our roots more or less directly tapped into those which arose from the soil of Nappa Hall, the bountiful mother of more illustrious Metcalfes.

This caused her to focus her research in a rather haphazard, dabbling way on the gentle aspect of the Metcalfe clan, leading her up the dale to Askrigg where she found a satisfying accumulation of Metcalfes in the parish registers. Some of these were knights and their ladies, others with less ostentation were styled esquire, but none of them, it now seems, were our Metcalfes. At least, none this side of the English Civil War were ours.

Fate has a curious way of closing the circle and just as it had led me inexorably to Northallerton as a student nurse in 1975, so providing a base camp for Aunty Kitty's earlier research, it has now led me back again in pursuit of the Metcalfe story. This is a story whose earthier truth is not to be found in Askrigg but in a triangle formed by Northallerton, Thirsk and Leyburn. More particularly, it has been found in the Northallerton public library and the County Records Office in Malpas Road; these have been my own base-camps for the past year of exploration.

In 1793 Jane Metcalfe of Crakehall, my four-times great-grandmother, gave birth to Margaret without first troubling the local clergy to marry her to the child's father. Margaret, by then living in Aiskew, followed her mother's example in 1811 and produced an 'illegitimate son' named Joseph. He then broke with tradition in marrying Ann Smith in 1836, about two months before she gave birth to William, the father of Auntie Kitty. (Ann, however, had already done enough on her own account to maintain the tradition, having given birth a year earlier to a daughter Jane, who subsequently assumed the Metcalfe name.)

William, born in early 1837, is something of a curiosity even by these standards, the information about him that I have gleaned seeming to ask more questions than it answers. There is no official evidence of him for a thirty-year period between the 1851 census and that of 1881. On the earlier date he is shown as living at home in what must have been a very crowded cottage in Little Fencote – in addition to his parents Joseph and Anne and his half-sister Jane, eight younger siblings were also in residence.

In 1881 he was again living with his parents but in Holtby Cottages, by the side of the Great North Road, near Holtby Hall. It was an address that Joseph and Ann had inhabited since at least 1871, one which William was to occupy for another decade and one which, in the years following the end of the Second World War, became part of the fabric of the new northbound carriageway of the A1 trunk road.

In May 1886, at the sprightly age of forty-nine, William took a wife, Catherine Ruddy, aged twenty-three, the daughter of an Irish bricklayer. Within a matter of weeks, she had produced their firstborn, suggesting that, in keeping with the family tradition, he had taken her unto himself somewhat earlier than 1886 and possibly accounting for him having shaved a decade off his age on the official record of the marriage. (It may have occurred to him that the reaction of a fifty-five-year-old Irish bricklayer to his young daughter's extramarital pregnancy might be slightly less intemperate if the guilty boyfriend was less

obviously his own contemporary.) This child was my grandfather Joseph, whose birth appears to have escaped the notice of the civil registrar, even though his baptism is recorded in the Great Fencote parish register. This absence of civil registration subsequently enabled him to perform his own age-reducing ruse in the post-war confusion of 1946, in order that he might carry on working until he was aged seventy-five.

Both he and his brother William also emulated their father's propensity for disappearance. My grandfather scooted off for twenty years at the turn of the century, reappearing in 1919, just before young William vanished permanently in 1922. The family believe, but without certain knowledge, that my grandfather's missing years were spent in the United States, but young William, like his father, remains an enigma. There simply appears to have been no trace of him since he walked out of the family home eighty years ago.

Or has there? Were the whimsical ruminations by Auntie Kitty through genteel Metcalfery an affectation which concealed a knowledge of the more unorthodox elements of the family history?

Perhaps. Following her death in 1983, we discovered among her belongings several unused presents, opened but still in their wrappings. Among these was one, that archetypal gift to maiden aunts and great aunts, Yardley's English Lavender Soap. It was accompanied by a card, 'To Auntie Kitty, With Love, Frances and family', written unmistakably in my mother's hand, except my mother is named after Auntie Kitty's older sister, Mabel. There is no Frances known in the family.

Aunty Kitty may have left us with no more knowledge of the family's past than did her older siblings or their forebears, but she appears to have left a new mystery.

Christopher J. Gallagher

5 Shops and Shopping

Shopping in Brompton in the 1940s

Walking around Brompton these days, one becomes very aware of how dependent the village is on the motor car and the nearby towns for shopping and the general requisites of modern life. Things were different when I was a child and the village had about twenty shops, which catered between them for most needs. Let me take you for a walk around the Brompton of the 1940s and we will visit each shop in turn.

We start off near the parish church of St Thomas, on the corner of Northallerton Road and Church View, where we visit Miss Lee's drapery shop. It is now the site of the only shop left in the village, but on our walk, Miss Lee is selling ladies' and children's wear and as you enter, you will most likely be bombarded with the strains of a Beethoven symphony played on the radio at full blast. Miss Lee is only the height of 'two penn'orth of copper' but she certainly likes her music 'big'. It is here that my mother buys her cotton pinafores and my white ankle socks. There is also a penny lending library.

We walk a little further on – just twenty yards or so – and call in at Milburn's fish and chip shop for a penn'orth of chips with scraps and salt and vinegar – a veritable feast in these days of food rationing. Mrs Milburn serves at the counter while Mr Milburn stokes the coal-fired range and deftly fries and tosses the fish and chips from the sizzling pan to the serving area. We children can hardly reach the top of the counter, it is so high.

Round the back of the church, near to the entrance to Wide Yard is Harry Smith's shop. The gleaming brass scales and weights are a fascinating sight, but there is always a funny smell in here. Can it be the fact that Harry sells, among a host of other things, paraffin and 'loose' vinegar? Paraffin at that time was a necessary commodity – used for cooking stoves and in some cases for lighting. It wasn't everyone who had taken on board the 'new-fangled' electricity and even though most of the houses in the area were wired up, many householders economized by still using paraffin lamps. Electric cookers were still a luxury item, only for the well-off, and many of the cottagers used the paraffin stove or coal-fired ovens for cooking. Harry also sells sweets, such as liquorice bootlaces and kali (a form of sherbert). Through the back of the shop we catch a glimpse of an old treadle sewing machine. Harry is also a tailor and will do all manner of alterations for a very modest sum. Outside the shop, fixed to the walls, are huge metal signs advertising Robin starch, Cherry Blossom shoe polish, Rinso washing powder and Brasso metal cleaner.

On past the factory gates and the house of Nurse Kitching, the village midwife, to Roxborough's shop. If we hadn't already bought our sweets at Harry Smith's, we could have got them here. Then past the manor house and we arrive at Boston's grocery store. Boston's have other shops in Northallerton and daily a supply of newly-baked bread, teacakes and fancy cakes is brought from their bakery there. Our present-day post office is sited in Boston's old shop. It is fascinating to

The green at Brompton.

watch the assistants make bags for sugar from sheets of blue paper. Similar bags are fashioned for flour from white paper. The butter and lard arrive in huge blocks and are then weighed into pounds and half-pounds as required. There is no self-service here and one has to wait patiently to be served while the smell of the newly-baked bread aggravates the taste buds.

Just a few yards further on, we arrive at another sweet shop, which also sells paraffin and 'loose' vinegar. (What did they do with all that acetic acid? Well don't forget, houses didn't have fridges and freezers in those days and a lot of things were pickled to preserve them). This shop is owned by the Walker family, who also run two buses and a coal merchant's business. Old Mrs Walker looks after the shop, which, incidentally, is very gloomy inside with a stone-flagged floor. Her sons, Sid and Rowley, manage and drive the buses and look after the coal business.

The post office is next door in premises that are now part of the Crown Inn. This business is run by the Cansfield family and Eric, the son, also has a taxi business which runs mainly between the village and Northallerton station. It is surprising how many people have more than one iron in the fire, perhaps due to the fact that one enterprise alone isn't sufficient to make a decent living.

The Crown Inn stands on one corner of Shop End and the Three Horse Shoes is on the opposite corner. The latter has a little sliding window just inside the front door, where you can take a jug and buy a pint or two of beer without actually going into the pub. This is useful for the women to use, as it still isn't acceptable for women to go into public houses. However, my mother does come here to pay my father's subscription to the Oddfellows club, which is a sort of early-day sick club.

Going up Cockpit Hill, we find the Co-operative Wholesale Stores, the CWS as it was

then known. This is a proper grocers shop with a bacon slicer, huge blocks of butter, lard and margarine, sacks of sugar and bins of flour standing on the floor. Here, as at Boston's, the assistants make up the sugar and flour bags and weigh out the commodities before tying up the bags with string which comes from a ball suspended from the ceiling. And, magic as magic, the money is put into a cylindrical container with the bill, all made out by hand. A handle is pulled and then it disappears, whoosh, to heavens knows where, before it returns with a 'plop' into a wire basket on the counter with the change all inside. Of course, to a child this is mystical. When the change is handed over, the customer also receives a small ticket on which is written your 'divi' number. As a customer of the Co-op, one is entitled to share in the profits and this is how your amount is determined. As you can imagine, this is a very busy shop and there are several men and women working here, all enveloped in huge white aprons. In addition, there is a delivery boy, who is kept busy taking out people's orders on the shop bike with its large wickerwork basket on the front. It can't have been too easy biking up Cockpit Hill or Bullamoor with that fully laden.

On top of Cockpit Hill, just before the village hall, is Mrs Dennis's sweet shop. It is very handy for me to call there on my way to school from Water End. One can get quite a lot of sweets for 1d and it is difficult to choose between lambs' tails or gob-stoppers. Perhaps I should have a ha'pporth of each.

Going down the hill towards Water End, we call in at Eric Naylor's bakery. Eric is a huge fat man and I understand his mother started off the business in Northallerton with a shop on the corner of Romanby Road and the High Street. Eric runs the Brompton shop. He is up very early every morning getting the coal-fired ovens hot enough to bake bread and teacakes. He then goes on to make cakes and pastries (his puff-pastry is out of this world)

Brompton church.

and he also serves in the shop. What a hard life! A large crusty loaf of bread is fourpence-halfpenny. Sometimes, we children gather up empty lemonade bottles, take them back to the shop and claim the 1d refund on them. When we have enough saved up, we go to Eric's and buy a loaf of lovely warm bread and then scrump it, tearing it to pieces with our hands and sharing it among us. Well it was in the days of rationing!

Opposite Eric's bakery is Alan Windress's newsagents shop. Alan is a cripple, possibly as a result of polio. I usually go with my mother on Saturday evenings to pay for our weekly newspapers. I think it costs about a shilling a week for the *Daily Express* each day and the *Darlington & Stockton Times* on a Saturday. If I have been very good all week, my mother may buy me a comic, perhaps the *Dandy* or *Beano*, or even the *Radio Fun* or *Film Fun*. Sometimes, I may get a copy of Enid Blyton's *Sunny Stories*.

The left-hand side of Water End has only one shop – Mrs Kipling's general store. Mrs Kipling's shop has a very strident bell, but even so, you may have to wait ages before she comes out to serve you, as she may be in her large back garden feeding the hens. Like Harry Smith's, this shop also boasts a beautiful set of brass scales. My mother gets her fresh yeast here for baking bread, which she does twice a week, usually on Tuesdays and Fridays. It is one of my jobs to look out for the DLC 'yeast man' coming so that we can get the yeast as fresh as possible. If it gets stale and dry, it does not rise the bread very well. I like to eat a little of the yeast and it is supposed to be good for you.

Crossing the middle bridge to the other side of Water End, we come to Walker's shop. This is a funny little building with a corrugated iron roof. Walker's is also a general store, selling a bit of everything.

Walking south again, we come to Polly Christon's fish and chip shop. Polly is very much a 'character' who always wears a sacking apron and a man's flat cap. She also has a fruit and vegetable round and keeps a horse and cart for this purpose – again, we have an example of more than one business being carried on by the same person. Polly also keeps hens, ducks and geese and those swimming on the beck are most likely hers. The ganders can be quite fierce in the spring when they have young goslings and I remember being chased by them more than once. I always try to make a detour to avoid going near them.

Polly's establishment overlooks Water End Green, where in addition to the geese and ducks on the beck, we see chickens in coops, cattle grazing and sometimes horses being exercised by Mr Lancaster or one of his grooms. Mr Lancaster lives near to Polly at Gordon House. As well as being a farmer, he deals in horses, buying them, breaking them in and then selling them on to the army. My father works for Mr Lancaster and so, for a time, did my brother, who tells me how he used to accompany the horses when they were moved around the country by train. Sometimes, when a fresh batch had been bought in, they would have to be walked from Northallerton station to the farm in Fullicar Lane. It was a distance of four miles – not a lot of fun with unbroken horses. Before we move on, I must tell you that to get her poultry from her back garden to the green, it is necessary for Polly to walk them through the hallway of her house. You can imagine what a mess they make!

Next to Polly's is Dowson's bread shop. The teacakes here are lovely and have shiny, brown tops. Dowson's also have a shop and bakery in Northallerton and Mr Dowson is known as 'Teacake Tommy'. Further on is Hoare's grocers and greengrocers. Old Mrs Hoare runs the shop, while Danny and Edgar, two of her sons, do the greengrocers' rounds. Mrs Hoare has a large family and will live to be over ninety. Alan and Eric Hoare are Edgar's sons and they have carried on the greengrocer's businesses to this day.

We have already visited Alan Windress's shop on Cockpit Hill, so now we go back to Shop End to call in at 'Sandy' Husthwaite's tobacconist's shop. Sandy sells beautiful brown pipes made from wood that looks like burnished chestnuts. He also has loose tobacco ready rubbed and huge twists of it which are sold by the ounce. In jars he has snuff, which I think is finely ground tobacco which is inhaled through the nostrils. This is weighed out with great precision and put into little paper twists. Sandy also sells the better sweets and not the 'kelter', as my mother calls it, which the other shops in the village sell. ('Kelter' is a local term for rubbish.)

Walking on past the big houses in which the mill owners live, and then past the Wesleyan chapel, we come to 'Rosy' Slater's butchers shop. 'Rosy' is a man, not a woman as you might think, and gets his name because of his lovely red face. He fattens cattle on land behind his shop and then slaughters them when they are ready.

Down the Pinfold and near the village 'lockup' is Spence's drapery shop. Mamma and Pappa Spence, as they are known, are quite old and rather forbidding. Most of their goods are kept wrapped up in brown paper parcels and 'Mamma' looks after the children's and ladies' wear while 'Pappa' sees to the gents' wear. My mother sometimes brings me here on Saturday evenings for a new pair of white socks to wear to Sunday school the next day or for a piece of material to make me a dress.

We then go next door into the barber's shop to get my hair cut. It is really a man's hairdressers and I much prefer to go to Northallerton to a proper ladies shop. I don't like having to sit on the wooden bench here along with the men and boys.

On the corner of The Pinfold is another butcher's shop – Mapplebeck's. Mr Mapplebeck

has a large bicycle with a huge wicker basket on the front and he delivers his orders around the village with this. We are now back where we started and you will see that we can get practically all we want in the village, although most people still go to Northallerton on market days by the local bus – probably as much for a social outing as anything.

In addition to the shops in the village, we also get numerous 'travellers' – for example, the onion seller, the scissor grinder, the lemonade man, the brush seller and the donkey stone man. 'What is a donkey stone?' you may ask. Well, it is a sort of sandstone which is wetted and then rubbed on stone doorsteps and windowsills to give them a decorative edge. We also get have the travelling representatives call from stores in Northallerton. Russell's the grocers send out a man once a fortnight collecting grocery orders which are then delivered later in the week. Clapham's, the smart clothing and furnishing store, send out their traveller about once every three months. He has large suitcases filled samples of clothing, linen and, nearer to Christmas, items like kid gloves and scarves, which will make suitable presents. Here again, you place your order with the man and it is later delivered to your door. This is very useful as no one has a car except for Mr Wilford, who owns one of the linen mills and Mr Lancaster, the horse dealer and farmer I have mentioned previously. They must be very rich!

Doreen Newcombe

Shopping in Northallerton in the 1950s

Shopping with Mum was great fun and the shops I remember visiting (with apologies to those forgotten), starting from the post office and going north, were Miss Sawdon's dress shop and Smithson's newsagents. Crossing over Romanby Road, you came to Eden's, the fruit and veg shop, the gas board and Woolworth's, with its lovely smell of warm salted peanuts, which you got in a greaseproof bag. The salt made the fingers sore! Woolworth's also sold an array of lampshades and lighting (Ikea, eat your heart out) and washing powders, as well as the usual goods. It had wooden floors.

Peggy Atkinson's was a hairdressers. I remember her cutting my hair with a 'razor' cut, with something that looked like a man's cut-throat razor. There was Mr Hodgson, the jeweller; Vitty's cycle shop was every child's dream at Christmas; Home and Colonial was where you could buy the Spam and potted meats mentioned before; Williams' tobacconists, Stockdale's butchers and Rogerson's, who sold wonderful pyjamas for children. They sold other things as well, but not as exciting to a child. They came in a cardboard box marked 'Land Of Nod'. The box was lovely and I think the pyjamas were too.

Russell's was a very special shop. It was a grocers and a treat was to have a cup of tea in the café, which was upstairs overlooking the pedestrian crossing. Inside the shop was the cashier's office, towards which your money was duly sucked through some great void of tubing travelling round the shop and from which your change returned. Often, though, Annie and later Evelyn and Mr Wake from Russell's would come first thing in a morning to your home and take your order. It would be delivered to your home, with the dried fruit in the blue paper bags.

Following on from Russell's was Barker's, who had another piped cash dispenser and was always the place to go for your shoes – suitably measured, of course. Tuft's – or was it Martin's – for watch repairs came next and then another hairdressers. They shared a doorway which, on entering, divided either side into two separate shops. Cleminson's and

Bickerdyke's the tailors followed and we have now arrived at the Central cinema, which was knocked down to make room for the entrance to the car park. It was known locally as the flea pit, but it also showed *The Tommy Steele Story* and I felt very grown up taken to watch it – or did the rumours make me feel more concerned about the fleas at the time?

There was a shop called Morgan's, which was the forerunner of catalogues, I think, since you had the option of paying weekly for clothes. York County Savings Bank was on the corner, but I remember the beck was open and ran parallel to the shops. The music shop was near the church, but I think that was in the sixties. It was run by a man called Johnny Briggs and his family, and as a teenager you could listen to your '45' single before buying.

Crossing over the road and turning back up the High Street, you came to the library – it shared the building with Hambleton District Council where the police station now is. People still lived in houses on the High Street and there was a fire in the house next door whilst Sunday school was taking place at the Wesleyan church, much to the excitement of the children.

The doctor's surgery was near the Rutson Hospital and you always got an appointment that day. You just went in and knew it was your turn after the man in the hat but before the lady sitting in the corner. Brilliant NHS!

Friarage Street held the beck, not to be paddled in on any account of course. The shops there had to be accessed via the footpaths over the beck. There was the baker's and a fish shop. Our famed Lewis and Cooper's of course and Archer's furniture shop and Anker's the ironmongers. A well-loved shop when I was a child was Miss Sadler's – another exciting trip because that is where new clothes were purchased, especially the Sunday school frocks!

Near the dress shop was Walker's (now Ottakar's). This was run in the sixties, if not

Cleminson's — one of the very few survivors from this 1950s ramble and still a treasure trove of things for the house.

before, by Mrs Cowper. Papers and stationery were in the front, then you went down a passage and turned right into the book room. Further down the passage was the toy department. Wonderful! I think Father Christmas was allowed to leave toys there until the big day arrived. Upstairs at Walker's was a little room at the front, which opened near Christmas to sell cards, mostly sold separately with the prices marked in pencil on the corner of the envelope. Opposite at the back of the store was the gift department, which was kept locked and opened on request. I know – I was the Christmas 'Saturday girl' in the sixties.

Fairburn's the chemists was next door. Clapham's had a department store (now Boyes). Miss Neasham's sweet shop was a delight, with everything a child could wish for on the floor, all open, and loads you could buy for 1d. I loved the Cadbury's chocolate penny bars which you sucked to a point.

Ronnie Smith's – or was it Boston's – had a baker's shop and to walk to town early on Good Friday and buy the hot cross buns as they came out of the oven from the bakehouse down the yard was wonderful! I loved to get home before they had cooled down.

On the corner of Zetland Street was the Miss O'Malleys', who sold homemade cakes in the front of the shop and lived in the back. They also sold penny loaves, miniatures of the real thing – just right for dollies tea parties. Wouldn't they have done well nowadays?

Crossing over Zetland Street going south must have been an area not much visited. Little legs must have got tired by then and were ready for turning down Zetland Street and going home, holding the treat of the day. I can't remember what was there, other than Swaledale Cleaners and at the bottom end of town the South End chapel.

I remember Naylor's garage, where you could buy petrol. Good Friday also saw a long queue of people out of Harrison's fish shop.

Wet fish was bought for dinner (at lunchtime!). We didn't seem to need fridges or freezers then.

Interspersed between all these shops were the usual banks and the many pubs Northallerton was famed for. I don't remember loads of building societies or estate agents. Perhaps Northallerton, being so much smaller then, didn't have as many houses to sell.

Running behind the shops on either side of the street were the yards where rows of houses were built. A lot of the yards were cobbled and some of the houses were still lived in the fifties. I think one of the last yards to be knocked down was when Barker's opened the Arcade. But notice that on the right, going down to the Applegarth, one of the shops still looks like a house – see if you can spot it. Apologies to any shopkeeper who was part of my fifties childhood and not mentioned. It was certainly not deliberate!

Valerie Plews

Shopping and business in Masham in the 1930s and '40s

There were two grocer's shops in the town. Watkinsons in Park Street, since taken over by the Co-op, and Brayshaws in Silver Street, which had a bakery behind and delivered bread and cakes by van to the outlying areas. There was a café adjoining.

There were two butchers in the town: Purves's, next to Brayshaws, and butcher Gill in Park Square. In my school days, he was known by another name by the local lads who did deliveries for him. When it came to remuneration, he said he would see them after and he became known as 'sees 'im after'. Actually, William Gill was not that bad. He sat behind us in church and provided us children with mint imperials to eat during the sermon. Also in Park Square was the former Mechanics Institute, more recently the Midland Bank.

Nearby were the two agricultural merchants in the town. Jack Broadley was the first. His employee, Ted Beasley, delivered feedingstuffs by horse and cart to outlying farms, combining this with his business as an insurance agent, which has been carried on by his family. I'Ansons had their mill between the Market Place and Park Square, with goods loaded and unloaded from the road. After the war, this business expanded and moved to Grewelthorpe Road.

In Park road, Mr Jameson senior had a small shop with a market garden behind. His son Edward developed a seedsman's business next door, delivering to farms over a wide area in a small Ford van. This business also expanded into foodstuffs and fertilizers, first in Leyburn road and then to an extensive manufacturing plant on the outskirts of the town. It is now managed by Edward's two sons.

The post office was next to the former Primitive Methodist chapel in Silver Street. The sorting office was a wooden building. The postmaster was Mr Bruce, whose parents and sister had a wool shop and a guesthouse further along the street where the post office is now. Mr Bruce Senior was for a large number of years superintendent of the Methodist Sunday school.

Further along Silver Street was Sturdy's cobblers shop and at the top of the bank was Mr Harrison's bungalow. He kept a few cows on a smallholding behind the gas works. Mr Harrison's son Harry ran a well-known cheese business, supplying shops over a wide area. He himself was supplied by Dales farmers and the more numerous cheese-making dairies in the area, including the local Masham Farmers Dairy. This was a co-operative formed by local farmers in the depression of the late 1920s. It supplied Wensleydale cheese for the maiden voyages of the liners *Queen Mary* and *Queen Elizabeth* in the 1930s.

Halfway along the avenue was the gas works where, until the arrival of North Sea gas, the town's gas was generated. This was overlooked by the North of England Malt Roasting Company, which is now the Black Sheep Brewery. When the Roasting Company was operational, we knew at Gebdykes when it was going to rain, because of the strong smell of malt. We also would see Captain Robert (Robbie) Theakston, manager of the local brewery, who had lost a leg in the First World War. He cycled through the town on a bicycle fitted with just one pedal and a fixed wheel drive.

H.H. Dyson

6 Wartime

Northallerton reflections on two World Wars

In exploring the colossal gamut of Northallerton's teeming history, time and time again the two World Wars of the twentieth century capture and re-capture attention. Obviously their importance and cataclysmic character partly explain this, but the fascination seems to lie deeper and in the very nature of the local people. It is indeed relevant that since medieval times, Northallerton and its district has been noted for the strong independence and spirit of its people.

The Great War of 1914-18 was so devastating in its terrible and indiscriminate loss of the nation's youthful patriotism-personified male generation that it demands and commands attention. Every city, town, village and hamlet was affected and the small area of Northallerton, Brompton and Romanby alone, by the Armistice of 11 November 1918, had a known loss of 146 young men.

These, the honoured dead, are etched in remembrance on the three solemnly grey war memorials – the appalling equivalent of around 500 of today's population. The enormity of the loss speaks for itself.

No wonder that Northallerton was stunned. No wonder that Mrs Hird, John Todd and others immediately gifted the Applegarth to the townspeople as a permanent memorial to the fallen. And no wonder that the dedication of the war memorial at the south-east corner of the churchyard on 6 August 1921 was the saddest and most poignant occasion in Northallerton's memory.

The North Riding county regiment, Alexandra Princess of Wales Own Yorkshire Regiment, the Green Howards, had borne the brunt of the local losses with a staggering 464 officers and 7,036 other ranks killed. The 4th (Territorial) Battalion had its headquarters at the drill hall, Northallerton, and their story encapsulates the attitude and spirit of the local combatants – the vast majority of whom were volunteers.

Private Thomas E. Banks, 4th Battalion Green Howards, killed at Ypres in May 1915. He was the first former Northallerton Grammar School pupil to fall.

The poignant dedication of the Northallerton war memorial, 6 August 1921.

At the outbreak of war in August 1914 the Green Howards 4th Battalion of Territorials (part-time soldiers) mustered quickly at Northallerton and early one morning marched off to war down South Parade to the railway station. The route was deeply lined with enthusiastic well-wishers. The 4th Battalion were around a thousand strong and often known as the 'Northallerton Territorials' because of their location. Led by their commanding officer, Lieutenant-Colonel Maurice Bell, they made a magnificent military spectacle swinging proudly along to the strident sounds of their band. Their khakied ranks stretched as far as the eye could see.

The majority never returned. Indeed, in April 1915 they were amongst the first Territorial soldiers thrust into the hell of modern warfare, which included the use for the first time by the Germans of the 'devilish' mustard gas. This was at the Second Battle of Ypres, when the 4th Battalion, along with fellow Durham and Northumberland Territorials, were hailed by the London Times as the 'Heroes of St Julien'. This was endorsed by the Army High Command, who highly praised the comparatively untrained part-time soldiers flung so hastily into battle to fill the gap where the Canadians had been decimated by the German gas attack. The 4th Battalion had stemmed the German advance at St Julien but their losses in men killed and men wounded were grave – a situation which continued throughout the war. At Northallerton, two more reserve 4th Battalions, around two thousand eager volunteers, were mustered. They were fed into the 4th Battalion on the western front, where they fought continuously and almost to a standstill with mounting losses.

For example, at the Somme on 14 September 1916, the 4th Battalion made history by accompanying 'tanks' into battle at Flers – the first time the British used the tank in warfare. But within seventeen days, the 4th Battalion had sustained 399 casualties, including eighty-two killed.

97

Finally, a war's-end count on 31 October 1918 recorded that there were only nine officers and eighty-nine other ranks left in the 4th Battalion.

Some random facts help to illustrate the war's local effects: in 1917, Mrs Buss, on hearing of the death of her husband Sergeant Major Buss, collapsed and died of a heart attack, leaving orphan children aged seven and three; in May 1918 thirty-two fatherless children at the National School received Savings Certificates; twelve Northallerton Grammar School ex-pupils fell, all barely out of their teens; and of Brompton's thirty-four young men who were killed, twenty-four were Green Howards and sixteen of these were with the 4th Battalion.

Overall, however, there was the repetitive theme of the commitment to and total acceptance by the young local men of doing their duty and going to fight for their country – an attitude of uncompromising patriotism.

Perhaps it is best summed up by Private William Leach of the 4th Battalion Green Howards, writing home after the St Julien action from the gas and shell-infested trenches at Ypres in May 1915 to his parents at New Row (now the Tesco site). He describes the fearful conditions where they could hardly put one foot in front of another, but ends on this typical and apt note: 'I am glad that so many of the lads of Northallerton and round about have answered the call of their country.'

Regarding the Second World War of 1939-45 and the Northallerton district, a different perspective is involved. Momentous events and world turmoil were interspersed with the vivid memories and experiences of a young boy living in wartime (almost war-stranded) Northallerton.

Our family, then of seven and soon to be eight children, were literally grouped around the wireless in our house in Thirsk Road, Northallerton, to hear the Prime Minister, Neville Chamberlain, deliver his doom-laden broadcast on 3 September 1939 to announce that Britain was at war with Germany. Even to a nearly-six-year-old, there was a vague sense

High Street south roadblock, 1940. Embattled Northallerton in defiant adversity.

that things were to be gravely different – and so it proved emphatically to be.

Almost simultaneously, the evacuees from Gateshead and Sunderland arrived in our market town midst to share some homes and all schools. Except for initial minor skirmishes of youthful territorial dispute, the newcomers who stayed (many quickly returned home) were soon absorbed and settled well.

Another unusual happening in late 1939 was the sudden appearance of long wooden huts (eight counted on clandestine exploration!) on the old show field behind the United Bus Station. Little did we know (or anyone else for that matter) that this was the advent of the eventually prestigious Friarage Hospital, which has been of incalculable importance and worth to Northallerton and its environs way up into the dales.

Mirroring most other local families, the elders in our family were thoroughly involved in the war effort: father, as assistant secretary to the North Riding Territorial Association, was responsible at the drill hall for organizing and equipping the Territorial soldiers (a crucial task after Dunkirk); sisters Rita and Paddy were part-time air-raid precaution control assistants; brother Bryan was a carrier of telegrams (vital in wartime) for the Post Office; and eldest brother Tommy, aged nineteen, was a sergeant in the Royal Engineers when wounded and evacuated at Dunkirk, took part in the invasions of North Africa, Sicily and Italy and finally was decorated with the Military Medal at the Battle of Cassino in 1944. Much of our 'family war' was inter-connected with our serving brother – again like all other such families.

At Northallerton, war conditions had revolutionized life. Everyone had to carry a National Identity Card and austerity ruled the day with the rationing of food, clothes, petrol, sweets (what a blow!) and so on. How mothers fed their families was a minor miracle

– ours very much included. Many heeded the Government exhortation to 'Dig For Victory' to produce their own food.

We dug up our lawn, planted vegetables and started to keep ducks – although the latter plan backfired, with the ducks becoming pets to us children and thus becoming sacrosanct from the fate of 'dressed bird' for Christmas dinner!

Sandbags were in great prominence protecting the main buildings – county hall, the police station, the town hall and drill hall. Air-raid shelters began to appear. Most homes had the Anderson outdoor underground shelter or the Morrison shelter in the house, resembling an oblong steel bed with a steel roof covering. All the schools eventually had brick-built shelters, some of which are still standing at the Allertonshire school.

To cover the possibility of gas attacks, by 1939 all the population were equipped with gas masks. Static water tanks in case of fire were sited at strategic points, notably in front of county hall. They were eventually converted into the present ornamental ponds.

To defend the town from invasion, concrete roadblocks were erected in 1940, narrowing the main road town entrances at the North End, East Road, Boroughbridge Road railway bridge, and the junction of the High Street with Thirsk Road and South Parade. Blockhouse sandbagged fortifications were built around the time in various fields.

The militaristic air in what now seemed like 'fortress Northallerton' was added to by continuous convoys of lorries and tanks with accompanying troops (shades of the medieval armies in the Anglo-Scottish warfare!). These troop movements were maximized after the Dunkirk evacuation in June 1940. Exhausted soldiers lay cheek by jowl on the grass verges of Thirsk Road and South Parade. The new military hospital (now the Friarage) received Dunkirk 'walking wounded' as its first-ever patients.

Sergeant Brian Kirk RAFVR Harsley Castle and ex-Northallerton Grammar School Hurricane Pilot, 74 Squadron. He died of wounds sustained flying in the Battle of Britain.

Finally in the wartime build-up, the Northern Vale of York became like a giant landing strip, with the opening of Royal Air Force bomber airfields. There were eight within the vicinity of Northallerton, where the military hospital tended to their casualties and became specifically Royal Air Force Hospital, Northallerton, on 1 January 1943.

Central to the Northallerton area was Royal Air Force Leeming, which opened in August 1940 with Whitley two-engined bombers, followed later by four-engined Halifax bombers. This was the commencement of a tremendous and continual rapport between Leeming and the surrounding local district. It was of great importance to morale, especially of the civilian population in those early dark days of the war, that the Leeming bomber crews, with their brave and tortuous missions to Nazi objectives, were carrying the war back to the Germans.

One of the biggest impacts on us children was the 'blackout' which aimed, when night fell, to eliminate all light which might attract enemy aircraft. Darkness enveloped the eerie town, making progress difficult and even fearful – especially for a young choirboy, who must have broken all records as he sped from the Parish church through the threatening High Street to the haven of home in Thirsk Road!

The air-raid warning siren, perched aloft on top of the county hall, had become an unwelcome intrusion on the nerves too – the first alert sounding on Monday 29 February 1940. The up-and-down wailing of the 'Alert' startled and took the breath away, whilst the welcome 'All clear' was a high-pitched one-noted long sound, which to us spelled relief.

We were virtually confined to the town and its immediate surroundings. Yet despite the shortages, austerity, adverse conditions and the unease of the war, there was an unmistakeable sense of confidence, fortitude and invincibility. Indeed, with Britain in adversity fighting almost alone against Hitler's Nazi Germany, the Northallerton district with backs to the wall evinced a spirit of unity, camaraderie, pride and belief in their cause which probably reflected the feelings of the nation. By common consent, this applied to all the generations, from the old to the young and from the men and women who flocked to volunteer for active service to those who were left keeping the home fires burning. It was a unique time.

There was only one actual bombing raid on Northallerton. On the night of 11 May 1941, a lone German bomber dropped four high explosive bombs across the town and a batch of incendiaries on and near the county hall. Only one person was killed: the unfortunate Private Joe Bolton RASC, who was on duty near the so-called 'White House' (now the Stanley Court site) on South Parade. It was the only building badly damaged in the attack.

Two other events stand out which shook the town, especially its young children. On 24 May 1941 the elite battleship of the British Fleet, HMS *Hood*, was sunk by the *Bismarck* with the loss of all 1,418 crew except for three survivors. The Applegarth Infants School (ages five to nine) had 'adopted' the *Hood* in 1939 and sent crates of 'comforts', and in many cases pupils had pen-pals to whom we wrote on the ship. Thus the news of the sinking of the ship was almost incomprehensible to young impressionable minds – wholly traumatic.

The Applegarth School featured in the next tragedy, which occurred on 2 December 1943. At 3 o'clock that afternoon, a Royal Canadian Air Force Halifax Bomber, which had been engaged in an air affiliation exercise with a Spitfire 6,000ft above Northallerton, developed a technical fault in the rudder and spiralled into the ground. It missed the Applegarth School

literally by yards, thundering over the roof and crashing just behind the school on Foster's bungalow and Springwell Lane. Its crew of seven, including its Canadian pilot, Flying Officer William J. Taylor, was lost. As flames and a thick pall of black smoke enveloped the area, people raced to the school from all over the town, believing it had been hit. Even though the children had escaped, the margin was so narrow that it left an indelible memory on all in Northallerton that day.

There were of course many compensatory highlights for the local people as the tide of war turned for the Allies in late 1942, including the visits of heroic Prime Minister Winston Churchill in 1942 and of King

Do you remember when the headlines said –

"No potatoes for this Sunday's joint"

While thousands of housewives enjoyed another little grumble, the wiser families who had dug for victory enjoyed their Sunday joint with all the potatoes and other vegetables they wanted. Learn from experience. To be sure of the family's veg-etables, you must grow them yourselves—women and older children as well as men. If you haven't a garden, ask your Local Council for an allotment. Start to

DIG FOR VICTORY NOW!

Government plea in 1939 for home-grown food.

Dedication on 31 October 1949 of Northallerton Grammar School war memorial to twenty fallen former pupils in the Second World War. The ceremony is being conducted by the Archbishop of York, Dr Cyril Garbutt.

VE Day street party celebrations, 8 May 1945. This is Rose Cottages, Malpas Road, Northallerton.

George VI and Princess Elizabeth on 11 August 1944; annual week-long savings campaigns such as 'Wings For Victory' (1943) and 'Salute the Soldier' (1944), which featured events, parades, bands and displays; and the heady news of successive Allied victories, culminating in 1945 with VE Day (8 May) and VJ Day (15 August).

On the other side of the coin were the casualties and especially those who made the supreme sacrifice. Their names were added to the respective war memorials – forty-one in Northallerton, nine in Brompton and eight in Romanby. Also remembered on the Northallerton memorial were the lost Canadian aircrew of No. 6 Bomber Group Royal Canadian Air Force, who had flown continually from the area since mid-1942. RCAF Leeming alone, for example, lost 903 aircrew in the last two years of the war.

Retrospectively, the mind inevitably turns back to those fraught early war days in embattled Northallerton. The country was in complete adversity but countered with the indomitable spirit and togetherness, which cemented the local North Yorkshire population together even in the face of supposed invasion.

Perhaps the fitting final words should go to an elderly lady from Richmond who, when questioned about the possibilities of a German invasion, replied:

'We're alreet. They'll stop 'em at Allerton afore they gets up 'ere!'

Michael H. Riordan

Some events of the last war

G.H. Bennions is presently a sprightly eighty-nine-year-old, who enjoys a daily walk and takes in events around him. His main complaint in life now is the fact that the DVLA at Swansea have decided to withdraw his driving licence, forcing him to part company with his beloved car.

This to him is ironic, as well as an irritation. Until 1977, 'Ben', as he prefers to be called, was flying a friend's Tiger Moth at air shows all over the country. He has only one eye, but his aerobatics were far in advance of most pilots with two eyes.

Ben learned to fly at RAF Cranwell in an AVRO 504. He was initially an apprentice Cadet and did an aircraft engineering course before becoming a pilot in 1929. By the time war started in September 1939, Ben was a fully-qualified and experienced pilot and was very proud and pleased when he was posted to one of the first squadrons to be equipped with the superb Supermarine Spitfires – 41 Squadron, based at Catterick.

During the Battle of Britain, Ben was in the thick of it, being shot down six times and in turn shooting down twelve German aircraft, mostly ME 109s.

The thirteenth, a yellow-nosed ME109, put a 20mm cannon shell through Ben's perspex

S/L GH BENNIONS /DFC

G.H. 'Ben' Bennions, DFC.

hood and shattered the instrument panel, sending pieces of flying metal into his face and piercing his left eye. By some miracle, Ben managed to bale out of his stricken aircraft, although to this day he cannot remember pulling the ripcord to open his parachute. He landed safely in a farmyard in Kent, where a farmer helped to save his life.

Despite having lost an eye and having had his face rebuilt by the celebrated plastic surgeon Sir Archibald McIndoe, Ben feels that life has been extremely benevolent to him on more than one occasion. And not only to him, but also to his wife and family. One of his flights of fate took place not over Biggin Hill, Duxford or the white cliffs of Dover but right over the village where he lives.

On the evening of 6 November 1939, two Spitfires flown by Bennions and F/O Overall took off from RAF Catterick. Their task was to locate a Whitly Bomber which had crashed somewhere in the area. The weather for the two pilots was far from ideal. Mist and thick patches of fog shrouded the airfield.

Overall took off ahead of Ben, who watched him gain height, then bank to the right and switch off his landing lights. He also noticed that for some inexplicable reason, the Spitfire was no longer gaining height, but was in fact descending right over the centre of Catterick village. Moments later there was a flash and a burst of flames from below. Ben realized that his colleague's aircraft had crashed into the heart of the village.

Ben returned to base, got into his car and raced down to the village, expecting the worst. As he turned into Mowbray Road, his

'Ben' Bennions with his car, before the DVLA pounced.

heart sank. Flames were leaping from his home – or so it appeared. As he got closer, he saw his wife Avis making frantic efforts to get into the blazing Spitfire, thinking it was Ben. She had to be restrained for her own safety. Every effort was made to recover the pilot, but in vain. He was not recovered until the arrival of the emergency services. Ben had the job of consoling his dear wife Avis, who was convinced that it was his Spitfire which had come down. By sheer irony of fate, his friend's aircraft had crashed into the garden and frontage of No. 1 Mowbray Road. The Bennions' house was next door at No. 2, and managed to come through with some scorching of the paintwork. No. 1, then belonging to the Hughes family, was damaged structurally, but by a miracle, no one was killed or injured.

The Canadian family of F/O Overall were so impressed by the efforts to save their beloved son and by the burial service held at Catterick that they offered to take the two Hughes children, Maureen and Tony, away from war-torn Britain and send them to school in Canada. This offer was accepted.

F/O Overall is buried in Catterick village cemetery along with many of his fellow countrymen. Today, there is little to indicate what happened on the evening of 6 November 1939 except for a nick in a wooden telegraph pole outside No. 1 Mowbray Road, where the wingtip of the Spitfire caught it. It may well have diverted the aircraft's path away from Ben's house at No. 2.

Despite losing an eye and treatment which lasted for two years, Ben later flew with the American Air Force in North Africa, teaching them how to fly Spitfires. He ended the war with the rank of Squadron Leader and was awarded the Distinguished Flying Cross and a mention in Dispatches.

Jim Davie

Wartime schooldays, 1940-46

How different a child's first introduction to school is today from my own experience way back in 1940. I well remember being taken along to Brompton County Primary School by my mother on that first morning (complete with gas mask in its little cardboard box), being registered and then left, abandoned – or so it seemed to me. There was no pre-school visit or preparation of any kind in those days. But I still survived!

There were approximately thirty children in the infant class. Some were old hands at the game, being six years old and very bossy with it. The number of pupils was high because of the evacuees from Hartlepool and Sunderland. Some had moved to the area with their families and others were billeted with local families while their parents remained back in their home towns. We were taught by Miss Thornton, who was past retirement age but had been retained because of staffing shortages due to the call-up of younger male teachers.

Our classroom had a coal fire with a huge fire-guard around it, which proved very useful for warming and drying our woollen gloves on those cold wartime winter mornings. Our daily third-of-a-pint of milk was often frozen solid in the glass bottles and these were placed near the fire to thaw out. Our desks were long wooden seats and tops at which about eight children sat in a continuous row. The windows of the room were high so that once one was in the room, all one saw of the outside world was sky.

I well remember on that first morning, a certain boy (who I won't embarrass by naming) cried the whole of the time, clinging so tightly to the door sneck that the teacher was unable to move him. In the end he wore himself out and fell asleep, still clutching at the sneck. The rest of us were too frightened to speak!

The routine of the day was very regimented. There was no freedom of movement around the room as there is in a primary school today, where children work and share equipment together. We just had to stay put and stay silent unless we were asked to answer a question or asked to go out to the teacher. On arrival in the morning, no matter what the weather, the children stayed outside on the playground until the bell summoned us to gather in lines, ready to march into the hall for morning assembly. Here again, we stood in lines according to age and sex, while we sung hymns and said our prayers.

Does my memory play tricks or was it always either 'All Things Bright and Beautiful' or 'There is a Green Hill Far Away'? After assembly, we marched to our classrooms for registration and the start of the day's work. There was a girl, one of the evacuees, who was always late, coming into the classroom when we were already embarked on our lessons. One day the teacher pinned a rabbit's tail to her rear-end in the hope of curing her bad timekeeping. Poor Peggy, it wasn't her fault.

We had playtime morning and afternoon. Morning play always started with our milk ration. We got a third-of-a-pint of very creamy milk issued free of charge. There was a cardboard top on the bottle with a hole in the middle through which you pushed your drinking straw. Mind you, in the summer, the freshness of the milk left something to be desired – remember fridges were not as commonplace as they are today. And, as I have already mentioned, in the winter months sometimes it was frozen solid, pushing the tops off the bottles.

Miss Lamb, the head teacher, was an extremely tall lady, at least 6ft in height with whiskers on her chin – funny the things you remember! She was pretty nifty with the cane or ruler when the occasion demanded, which seemed to be fairly frequently. Both boys and girls were either given the ruler or caned. A cane coming down from that height certainly

left its mark, but of course we dare not tell our parents when we had been punished. We would only have got more when we went home. One wet lunchtime, when we had to stay indoors for playtime, I went to the toilet across the yard without asking to leave the room. Upon my return I was caned on both hands for going without permission. I still blush at the indignity of it, but such was the discipline at that time.

As the country was at war during my years at Brompton school, that in itself created unusual circumstances. For instance, all the windows were criss-crossed with brown sticky paper to prevent glass fragments flying about should the building be bombed. Of course we had to take our gas masks with us everywhere we went. These were sometimes carried in their original cardboard boxes with string through the sides so that they could be slung over the shoulder. The better-off among us had special waterproof cases. The mobile 'gas chamber' used to visit periodically and then we had to don our masks and go into the darkened van, where I presume some gas was released. On coming out, our masks were examined and the people in charge were able to tell if they were functioning properly by looking at the crystals in the base. Fortunately, the gas masks were never needed in a real gas attack.

On one occasion, the air-raid warning siren sounded and we all had to get under our desks for cover. We sang songs while crouching there – not an easy feat! However, it must have been a false alarm as I can't recall any action. A few bombs were dropped in the area on another occasion. South Parade in Northallerton had a direct hit one night and some small bombs were dropped on Brompton Banks. One sunny Sunday afternoon, a plane crashed in some fields alongside Stokesley Road – almost directly behind the house where I now live. Unfortunately, the pilot was killed.

Progression through school depended on ability as well as age and I was fortunate to find myself in the 'top class' at the age of ten. Mental arithmetic tests were held every Friday morning and where you sat in the class depended on your test results that week. 'How many inches are there in three yards, two feet and ten inches?' and 'How much do ten dozen eggs cost at one and elevenpence halfpenny a dozen?' were typical of the questions we were asked. The pupils with the highest marks sat in the back row and those with the lowest sat in the front row, under the direct eye of Miss Lamb. Those of us with a good memory got that we could memorize the questions and the answers, but then, isn't having a good memory what mental arithmetic is all about? Tables and poetry were also learned by rote and I can still recite, word for word, poems like John Masefield's 'Cargoes', Wordsworth's 'Daffodils' and Keats' 'Ode To Autumn'.

Brompton school had two playgrounds, or 'yards' as we called them: one for the boys and one for the girls. The toilets were outside, across the yard. The distance required that one set off in good time – providing one got permission to go, of course! Our playground games seemed to follow the seasons. We always had snow and there was sliding and snowballing in winter. Sliding required that you had your leather-soled shoes strengthened with segs – flat-topped, metal three-pronged nails. Otherwise, your shoes quickly wore out. Springtime saw the emergence of whips and tops and marbles for the boys. In summer, out came the skipping ropes and the chanted rhymes that went with them: 'Pitch, Patch, Pepper' and 'All In Together Girls'. In autumn, when the days started to get colder, we had to run around more to keep warm, so Tigs became the order of the day. Our P.E. lessons, such as they were, often took place on the playground. We were always split into four teams – blue, red, green and yellow. I can remember dumpy little Miss Bendelow, in her tight tweed skirt, trying to show us how to bend and stretch and jump our feet apart. Not for us the sophisticated equipment of today. We only had hoops and skipping ropes.

Regular visits from the 'nit nurse' were also a feature of school life. Local mothers always blamed the evacuees for the infestations of head-lice. Oh, the shame of having your name put down in the nurse's little black book and then suffering the indignity and pain of the small-tooth comb and the Derbac shampoo.

The culmination of one's years at primary school was the dreaded Scholarship Examination, or Eleven-Plus as it was later known. The Scholarship was taken in two parts. The first part was taken at your primary school and if you passed, you then went on to take the second part at the grammar school in Northallerton on a Saturday morning. Success or failure in this examination determined whether you went on to the grammar school or to the Allertonshire Secondary Modern School.

The school dentist visited school the day before I was due to sit the second half of the examination and I had to have five teeth taken out under anaesthetic – not the best of preparations for this important event. As a special concession, Miss Lamb allowed me to go home after I had had my teeth extracted and this was indeed preferential treatment. You were usually left to recover at school and then to go home at the appointed time. We were given three new pencils to take along to the exam and mine were brought to my house after school by two other girls who were also taking the test. They knocked at my door, clutching their own new pencils and handed me mine. I couldn't help noticing that the points on their pencils were much sharper than mine. Despite such a disadvantage, I gained my scholarship and they failed. Such is justice as seen through the eyes of an eleven-year-old.

And so my years at Brompton school came to an end, as had the Second World War. We had been very lucky, living out in the country as we did. We didn't experience much of the action and hardship that many others suffered and I don't recall the war having too much effect on my childhood. Perhaps we took it all for granted as, being so young when it started, we couldn't remember much else. We always seemed to have plenty to eat, thanks to the school dinners and the fact that my father worked on a farm and brought home lots of rabbits which my mother made into delicious rabbit pies. Perhaps we didn't have all the toys, clothes and equipment that children have today, but we made our own amusement and managed to have a happy childhood.

Doreen Newcombe

The 4th Battalion – Yorkshire Regiment (Green Howards) at the Beginning of the First World War

The shockwaves of the shots which killed the Archduke Franz Ferdinand of Austria in Sarajevo in June 1914 swept across Europe and disturbed the peace of Northallerton at the beginning of August. The town housed the headquarters of the 4th Battalion of the Yorkshire Regiment in the drill hall on Thirsk Road. This battalion was a territorial unit, which at the time had no obligation to serve overseas.

When hostilities broke out on 4 August 1914 they were at Conwy in north Wales attending their annual camp. They were ordered to return home immediately and report to headquarters in accordance with mobilization plans. Such was the war fever that gripped the town's population that crowds of people waited at the station to greet the returning 'Terriers', many waiting for the last train at 11.30 p.m. on the Monday evening.

Orders had been issued requiring the local publicans to provide accommodation for the men. The thirty men who arrived on the last train were told to go to their own homes for the night and to report to headquarters in the morning, as were the men of the Thirsk, Helperby and Bedale Detachments. There was a great deal of activity in the town the next morning, with the local unit much in evidence. The centre of operations was the drill hall, which had only been completed two years earlier. Horse-drawn carts worked between there and the station transporting essential supplies and equipment. So great was the demand for billets for the troops that fifty men slept in the gymnasium of the grammar school, and in September the other schools were used.

The closure of the new council school, now the Applegarth Primary School, is recorded in the school Log Book by the headmistress, Miss H.M. Smith, who wrote on 9 September, 1914: 'The school has been closed this afternoon until further notice. It is required for the purpose of billeting troops.' Other buildings that were taken over for the same purpose were the town hall, the National School and the Old Court House (to the north of the prison and now demolished). The town was in a state of excited commotion, with the residents watching the marching soldiers from doorways and other vantage points. By the middle of that Tuesday, the area round the drill hall was extremely busy with baggage piled up both inside and outside the building. Armed sentries with fixed bayonets mounted guard outside while two .303 machine-guns, in service with the British Army since the Matabele War of 1893-94, flanked the doorway. Inside the hall, bayonets were being sharpened, equipment sorted and the soldiers kitted out with haversacks, rifles and bayonets, ready to be formed into detachments ready for action.

Northallerton echoed to the sound of

Depot Company, 4th Battalion Yorkshire Regiment under Captain Constantine.

4th Battalion Yorkshire Regiment at Richmond Camp.

drums and bugles as, watched by the excited inhabitants, the troops paraded along the High Street and the cobble-flanked Market Place. The public places were hives of activity until late in the evening when people settled down, after which the streets were deserted except for the sentries on guard. The peace of the night was short-lived, however, for at 4.45 a.m., the sleepy inhabitants were roused from their slumbers by a bugle band marching down the streets, calling the troops for early duty. For the soldiers, life was busy and varied. Many of them lived in tents in the grounds of the grammar school and the surrounding fields. What is now Hutchison Drive, a quiet residential road, was the canvas home for some. An army field kitchen was established behind the grammar school to provide meals for the hungry men – bacon and fried bread for breakfast. The midday meal was described by one veteran as a 'lash-up' – meat and vegetables dished up in the form of a stew. At meal times, it was the job of the duty orderly to collect the 'dixies' (large metal cooking pans, containing food for the eleven men who lived in each tent) and to be responsible for the washing up afterwards. This task had to be accomplished in cold water and as there were no detergents in those days, it was difficult to get them thoroughly clean. The tea at teatime, made in the same container, could therefore be flavoured with the previous meal, with at times a layer of grease floating on the surface.

In general, the soldiers began with the 6.30 a.m. reveille, followed by a wash in cold water and the regulation shave. Beds would be tidied away and the kit made ready for inspection. After that, the day's training began. Fitness is essential for a soldier, so physical training was a regular activity with exercises designed to strengthen muscles and improve stamina. Part of Friday was set aside for a route march. The

On the other side of this postcard, dated 30 September 1914, Edie has written, 'It's lovely – am having tea with your Billie. Been watching the boys playing soldiers'. 'Billie' then breaks in to add, 'kind regards from Private Davis of the 4th. I ought to have been writing. You'll know the reason why. Bill'.

companies formed up outside headquarters and set off along Crosby Road, then headed up Sandy Bank to Thornton-le-Beans and returned to Northallerton in time for dinner.

In the early days, the Battalion was armed with the Long Lee Enfield rifle, the new short version being required for the fighting units. To improve the standards of marksmanship for which the British Army was renowned, frequent practice was undertaken on the 600-yard range on Greenhowsyke Lane. This area was later used as the gardens for the prison. Trench digging was also practised. For this, the men were marched out to Warlaby to dig a trench. It was no great hardship to those used to manual work, but it caused blisters and aching backs for those who were not. All this for 3s 6d a week.

In September a severe storm swept through, wreaking havoc among the tents. One marquee accommodating some fifty or sixty men was completely swept away, leaving them without shelter. Action had to be taken. The top floor of the prison was cleared of prisoners and the soldiers crammed in seven to a cell – less comfort than that enjoyed by the regular inmates.

All this military activity had its effects on the town. Education was disrupted for all ages. The closure of the schools meant that other places had to be found and parents were asked to pay 3d a week for their education. Some children missed school because their parents either could or would not pay. The council expressed their concern at the loss of education. Another cause of concern was £300 lost in fees at the grammar school. The Education Authority allowed the Military rent-free use of the council school, but required payment for the heat and light costs incurred.

The local members of the Red Cross were busy converting a committee room in the county hall and a waiting room at the station into an improvized hospital. Sheets and bedding were borrowed from the householders to equip the makeshift wards.

In October, the chief constable of the North Riding, Major Sir Robert Lister-Bower, KBE, CMG, banned the billeting of troops in private houses due to the severe overcrowding that was occurring. With some extra thousand people with money to spend, the shops and public houses gained financially.

In early 1915, a second reserve battalion was formed and the Zion Congregational schoolroom was commandeered for use as a social room for the troops. The training programme was accelerated and with supplies of the Short Lee Enfield rifle becoming available, more shooting practice was carried out. Young men were keen to join up and units were being formed so rapidly that uniforms were not readily available and civilian clothes had to be worn.

In April 1915, the battalions moved from Northallerton. On the last evening, houses were crowded as the troops and townspeople

Part of the Northallerton war memorial.

111

said goodbye. On the morning of departure, Reveille was at 3.00 a.m., with breakfast at 3.30. B and C Companies marched to the station at 5.00, followed by A and D Companies at 6.45, who were accompanied by the commanding officer, Colonel Wharton. They were given an enthusiastic send-off by a large number who rose early especially.

Slowly the town returned to normality. On 3 May 1915 the head of the National Council School recorded in the Log Book: 'The school has reopened this morning.' Many of the men who marched off so proudly that morning now lie in the soil of France. Of those who returned, many bore the scars of battle. In the surge of patriotism that swept the country in late 1914, one mother is reported in the *Darlington & Stockton Times* as giving this advice to her son:

'My boy, I don't want you to go – but if I were you, I should go...'

Phil Pidd

Life as a land girl
Prize-winning entry

I had spent my early years in the cotton town of Burnley, living with my father and grandmother. My mother had died when I was a small child. Although I wanted to attend Lancashire School of Agriculture, my grandmother would not let me leave home because she suffered from a debilitating illness. So I underwent secretarial training. When grandmother died, my father and I went to live with his brother's family, helping to run a smallholding at Staithes.

At the outbreak of war on 3 September 1939, I was eighteen and, although I was enjoying learning drama in my spare time and teaching at Sunday school, I was unsettled because there were no office jobs available in the area. Then six evacuee children were billeted with us, accompanied by a dragon of a foster-mother who totally upset the atmosphere in our family home. I felt that I had to escape just at the time that young people were being asked to support the war effort by joining one of the services.

Working on the land appealed most to me so, with my father's blessing, I travelled to Guisborough Hall and applied to join the Women's Land Army. It had been re-formed to enable women to replace agricultural labourers who had been called up. I was fortunate to be accepted for a place at Askham Bryan Agricultural College near York, starting in the first week of January 1940. It was a lonely journey into the unknown.

I felt very lost as I walked up the imposing drive, but my trepidation soon disappeared when I met the other fourteen Yorkshire girls on my course. We all lived and trained at the college and despite being from all walks of life, got on very well. In the evenings we attended lectures (I still have some of my notes) by good tutors who also guided our practical learning during the day. First, we were taught the daily basic farming chores, such as milking cows and feeding chickens and pigs. Then we progressed to churning and making butter, dressing chickens and even dismantling a tractor and then putting it back together again. The highlights of our occasional leisure time were college dances partnered very decorously by the tutors, and playing rugby when the ground was not too hard. In fact such outdoor fun was infrequent as the bitter cold of that icy winter made the river Ouse freeze over and curtailed the bus service between York and Tadcaster. I remember that one day we tried to snag (top and tail) mangels for animal feed, but the earth was so solid that the task proved impossible.

Although I really enjoyed my training, it did not prepare me for the reality of the long hours of heavy work on an operational farm. On completion of our training, one of my

Clare Jobling loading corn for the stack-yard, 1940. The horse was called Topsy.

friends and I were sent together to live in and help on a farm in lower Wensleydale. Although the farmer was kind, his wife did not feed us well and when we were allowed a break, we used to walk the five miles to Leyburn and back simply to buy extra food. However, after only six months, the farmer decided that there would not be enough work to retain us over the winter and we were both reallocated. I was drafted on my own to a large farm at Danby Wiske, where I dined and slept with the family. Piped water and electricity did not arrive until the early fifties, so all water had to be carried in buckets from the pump. The buildings were lit with paraffin lamps, and hurricane lamps were carried in unlit areas. My principal work involved dairying, using a small portable machine which milked one cow at a time, then stripping by hand the spare milk that any cow had not let down and

washing all utensils to keep them spotlessly clean. The milk was transferred from the milking unit by pail to the milk house and poured into a receiving pan. This channelled the milk over a cooler through which cold water was flowing, through a sieve to remove any impurities and into 12 or 15-gallon churns. By modern standards, dairy herds were very small, between one and two dozen animals.

When full, the churns were extremely heavy for a slightly-built girl. They were loaded for me on to a pony and trap and I drove them to the nearby railway station for transport to the dairy. There I was helped to unload by the station porter or by any other farmer delivering his own milk. Once the grass stopped growing, the dairy cows were tethered in byres all winter. Then, in addition to milking twice a day, my daily tasks included ensuring that each animal had enough feed and water, and twice cleaning out the byres and washing down the walls behind. To fatten beef cattle, I chopped up mangels, swedes and sometimes straw by turning the handles on small chopping machines.

Once spring returned, the beasts were turned out to pasture, but the grass in some fields was allowed to grow to be cut and stored for winter feed. Hay making in both early and late summer was relatively pleasant work. The long grass was cut by machine in sunny weather and left on the ground for several days to start drying off, as wet grass would go rotten. Then we raked it up into small round heaps called 'cocks' to continue the drying process. Finally, we loaded the cocks onto a horse-drawn cart or bogey and took them to the stack-yard. There they were built into haystacks, which were thatched to shed rain. Any surplus was sold to hay buyers. Come

A 1942 studio photograph of Clare in her Women's Land Army uniform.

winter, the stack would be cut into with a hay spade and the hay carted into the cow byres and stables, horses having not yet been replaced by tractors.

Harvesting corn was an altogether harder task, while threshing to separate the grain from the chaff and straw required dedicated teamwork. In those days, the quickest way to cut corn was with a binder customarily drawn by three horses. If the gap between corn and hedge was too small for the horses, one or two men with scythes would first mow an access road for them around the field. I followed behind collecting the cut corn into sheaves, which I bound with plaited stalks and stacked against the hedgerow out of harm's way. Once the access was clear, the horses pulled the binder round and round the field in ever-diminishing circles, ejecting bound sheaves in its wake. I constantly followed, gathering ten or twelve sheaves at a time to stand in a series of stooks to dry out. When the stooks were considered to be dry enough, I loaded them onto a horse-drawn cart or flat-topped bogey and transported them to the stack yard. I had a very good teacher who showed me the best way to load sheaves so that they were evenly balanced on a cart. I was proud of my ability to build good straight loads. The sheaves were stacked either in an open-sided Dutch barn or in thatched stacks to be kept dry for threshing.

The main East Coast Railway ran through that farm and one day, as I was leading a horse pulling a cart loaded with sheaves, I heard a northbound train approaching and looked up to watch it pass. Imagine my amazement when I saw my own father gazing out of a window! We spotted each other at the same time and both waved furiously for a few brief moments before passing out of each other's sight. It was a magical moment for us both, having been separated for so long by the war.

Another powerful memory is of a frightening event. One Monday, a colleague and I were working in a pasture field when we

Taking a 3 o'clock break for refreshments while using a horse-drawn binder.

heard an aeroplane, and it was low enough for us to recognize it as a German bomber. We ducked automatically as it flew overhead and it was only a short time later that we heard explosions and assumed that bombs had been dropped not far away. Then we saw the bomber returning, still flying low. Fearing it might attack us this time, we ran and cowered in a flimsy shelter of hedge – but it chose to ignore us. We later heard that it had bombed Leeming aerodrome and damaged several of our fighter planes on the ground.

For threshing day, a contractor was hired to bring a huge machine drawn by a heavy steam engine, which ploughed deep ruts in farm tracks and stack yards, especially when the ground was soft. In addition to the contractor and his assistant, a team of twelve to fifteen farm workers loaned by other farmers was

necessary to carry out the sequential tasks involved. The threshing machine was powered by the steam engine, which was tended by the contractor and needed supplying with coal and buckets of water all day. Sheaves of corn were pitchforked off the stack or out of the barn and thrown up on to the top of the machine. There, the straw bands were cut and the loose corn was fed into the thresher. The latter automatically tied the straw into battens, which were built into new stacks to provide indoor animal bedding. The freshly threshed grain pouring out of the machine was caught in sacks weighing 12 stones for oats, 16 for barley and 18 for wheat, and stored in the granary. Fortunately, I was usually given one of the lighter jobs like carrying water, cutting the bands, forking battens or 'cowling the chaff'

– the dusty task of sweeping up the chaff that constantly accumulated underneath and around the thresher. All the manual work involved in threshing was extremely strenuous, but the ready banter between the workers helped things along.

No chemicals were used during the war years and all other work had to be done manually, like digging up dock plants, scything down thistles and nettles and burning thorns after hedges had been slashed. In season, I picked field mushrooms, which were sold in Darlington market. It was a very busy life but, whenever farm duties allowed, I attended both the local Methodist chapel and the parish church. In fact I was confirmed in the latter, having attended classes in the rector's bedroom, as he was disabled. Whenever I was free on a Saturday, I would walk into Northallerton or take the bus to Darlington for a change of pace.

I worked on that farm for two and a half years, and then on two other farms in Danby Wiske, always being treated as a member of the family, until the end of the war. The transfers occurred after I was sent home to recover, first from a badly-infected hand and secondly from ringworm caught from infected calves. The main entertainment in those wartime days was the occasional dance at the Village Institute, when the farming community, depleted of men of fighting age, was supplemented by servicemen stationed at local mansions that had been requisitioned. The most memorable, of course, was that organized to celebrate VE Day, when a huge bonfire was lit on the village green after all those years of blackout.

A few years later, I married a local farmer and have lived at Danby Wiske ever since. I've remained friendly with the families for whom I worked during those difficult times and I am extremely proud of my Women's Land Army Five Years Shield.

Clare Jobling

Plane crash in wartime winter

The second week of January 1942 brought heavy snow. By the twelfth day, the snow lay, as Good King Wenceslas would have said 'deep and crisp and even'. Mrs Annie Sedgwick of Brick House Farm had commenced her chick-hatching business and had hundreds of chicks in their wooden hen huts, heated by paraffin heaters. A keen frost had followed the snow and while the snowploughs had cleared the roads to some extent there were frozen lumps of snow high on the verges.

In these circumstances the Sedgwick family went to bed on 15 January 1942. Annie Sedgwick had made the compulsory blackouts for their bedroom window from old poultry-feed bags reinforced with wooden laths and, although crude, they were effective for their purpose. The couple and their eight-year-old son were sharing a room and Mr Godfrey Sedgwick was sleeping soundly. He was quite happy to leave the worrying and most of the work to his wife. Annie Sedgwick dropped into fitful sleep, wondering if her chicks were warm enough during the freezing night and hoping the paraffin lamps were burning safely.

Suddenly, Annie was aware that the bedroom was lit up from the outside in spite of the blackout at the window. Although the poultry-feed bags served their purpose as blackouts, they were not completely opaque and now the window was brilliantly lit, as brightly as sunlight. Annie shook the sleeping Godfrey, who muttered, 'Oh, it's only the moon', but by this time she was at the window and having removed the blackout, she was joined at the window by her protesting husband. The scene which greeted them was terrifying: the whole snow-covered landscape was lit by a brilliant pink light, almost brighter than a summer day. All Annie's poultry houses, the other farm buildings, the hedges and trees stood in an unearthly pink brilliance. Northallerton church tower, a mile away, was clearly visible – also pink – and even Bullamoor two miles away with its farmhouses and fields stood clear and ghastly in a pink light. A cockerel was lustily crowing as if to celebrate a false and terrible dawn.

The source of this strange light was hidden from the terrified couple by the farm buildings, so Godfrey quickly dressed and apprehensively went out into the yard to investigate. Annie grabbed her young son from his bed and took him downstairs as she had been instructed to do by the ARP. Once out of the house, Godfrey could see that the source of the light was an enormous fire about 100 yards away across the Darlington Road. He soon realized that the farm was in no immediate danger from the fire, but he could feel the heat on his face as he looked incredulously at the red-coloured flames reaching hundreds of feet into the air.

Within a few minutes, the flames began to die down a little and Godfrey wondered what to do. He was not by any means a brave man and although he had been conscripted in the First World War, he had been found unfit for active service and spent the war years in the Royal Army Veterinary Corps attending to sick horses. The flames were now receding and the brilliant pink light was changed into a fitful yellowish colour emanating from a point where a strange spluttering sound of burning oil on water was mixed with the popping of mild explosions.

Godfrey's stomach was churning and his mouth was dry, but he felt that he must somehow find out what was happening. As he made his way across the Darlington Road, he began to panic. What was happening? Was it a bomb? Was it an aeroplane crash? Or worse? By the time he reached the road he was in absolute terror. The dying flames were making grotesque shadows from the trees and hedges and he imagined German soldiers pointing rifles at him or another blaze consuming him – or worse. He had never felt so lonely in his life.

The field gate onto the Darlington Road was almost covered with frozen snow and as Godfrey was climbing over it, even more terror struck him. He could hear voices in the flickering shadows. Transfixed with fear half over the gate, he jumped violently as a voice called out 'It's a plane down, mate'. Two lorry drivers had been travelling south on the Darlington Road and they had stopped and quite sensibly switched off their lights. The three men stood on the snow-covered road and watched the flames die down and the explosions become less frequent. They were joined by another farmer, Harold Swalwell, who had also been awakened by the flames and had walked along the road to investigate. By now, the aircraft's fuel was exhausted and only the combustible parts of the fuselage were still burning. A blazing tyre was forming a beacon to light the scene.

They were joined by John Walker, a younger farmer from Highfield Farm and all agreed that none of them had heard the sound of the crash. All had only seen the fire. They now began to approach the blazing wreckage and as the roaring of the flames died away, they became of other sounds in the still night. There was the drone of aircraft overhead, which they hoped were friendly and the cockerel was still in full voice. One of the lorry drivers said 'I wonder if it's one of ours. I doubt they'll all be dead, but we'll have to go and see'.

Very cautiously, they approached the wreckage and were soon startled to hear a voice and some moaning. In a patch of half-melted snow were two aircrew. One was lying silently on his back with blood issuing from nose and mouth. The other was in a sitting position with blood covering his torn uniform and repeating over and over again, 'OK, I'll take her round again'. 'Good God!' said one of the lorry drivers, 'These poor buggers want to be in hospital!'

Nowadays an ambulance would have dealt with such a circumstance, but in 1942 there were few telephones and on this occasion the nearest telephone was in Northallerton. One or two more lorries were now stopping on the road, the drivers coming to help and by removing the field gate, an improvised stretcher was made. One driver shouted 'My wagon's empty. Get 'em on to it. And there should be seven of 'em somewhere'. How he knew this, no-one saw fit to question, but a search duly found six airmen just alive and one still in the remains of the fuselage, barely recognizable as anything human with his uniform completely burned away and his arms and legs reduced to stumps.

The six crew who were still alive were loaded unceremoniously on the back of the lorry in the freezing cold and transported to the Friarage, or as it was then known, 'Base' Hospital. Five of them either died on the back of the lorry or soon after arrival at the hospital. One, the pilot, survived for some weeks, still from time to time murmuring 'OK, I'll take her round again'. It seems as if he must have had some radio contact with his base shortly before the crash. The actual cause of the crash was never discovered.

The three farmers were in a state of shock for some days afterwards and very rarely mentioned it for the rest of their lives. Today the crash site is just an ordinary farm field and the whole episode forgotten. The airmen who died were:-

Sgt T. Cowan, RAF
Sgt H.K. Taylor, RAF
Sgt J.C. Bradley, RAF
P/O V.L. Brice, RCAF
P/O M. von Dadelszen, RNZAF
F/Sgt D. Savage, RCAF
Sgt M.S. Schneider, RCAF (the pilot)

The aircraft was a Halifax B. Mk II, No. L 9622 and had taken off from Leeming at 6.12 p.m.

on a bombing mission to Hamburg. It was on its way back to base when it crashed.

J.F. Sedgwick

Romanby Women's Institute – the war years

The formation meeting for Romanby Women's Institute was held in Romanby school on 26 September 1928, when about eighty ladies voted to form an institute. The very first meeting was held at the Dairy Institute, Northallerton, on 23 October 1928. At the June meeting in 1931, a building fund was started as members felt the need for their own permanent meeting place. After a lot of hard work at fundraising, the dream was finally realized when the new hall was opened on 12 April 1939 with afternoon tea and an evening concert.

The first rumblings of war were heard in Romanby Women's Institute at the very first meeting in the new hall on 18 April 1939. Yorkshire County were concerned with National Service and wrote asking for volunteers to attend classes for cooking using improvised stoves, camp kitchens and so on. Eight of our members agreed to go. Also, as the country seemed on the verge of war, the National Federation of Women's Institutes formed a produce guild. This had been mooted as early as 1927. The Ministry of Agriculture contributed £500. This guild, which lasted until 1972, was responsible during the war for providing members with 140,000 fruit bushes and 134,000 packets of vegetable seeds. Romanby decided to form its own produce guild.

At the meeting in May, classes were arranged during June and July for the making of bandages. No further meetings were held until after war was declared. The Women's Institute met again on 21 October 1939 at 2.30 p.m. and decided not to hold an annual meeting because of the war. The present committee would remain in office for the next year. Members' night would be in November with crazy whist and a sing-along. At the December meeting, some members offered to make shirts for the Polish forces. It was also arranged to invite the soldiers from Church House and White House to the Christmas party on 26 December.

At the beginning of 1940, the January meeting agreed to hold social evenings for the forces once a fortnight. This was a great success so members decided that the proceeds would be used to buy wool to knit up for servicemen. It was in 1939 that the Women's Institute nationally was asked by the Ministry of Agriculture to organize a cooperative fruit preservation scheme to save and make use of surplus fruit. *Home and Country*, the WI magazine, set the tone for the jam-makers of 1940 with the slogan 'Produce – Preserve', saying, 'these are the watchwords of the Women's Institute in these

summer days of stress'. In two months, the number of jam and preservation centres shot up from 157 to 1,855.

Meanwhile, Romanby WI decided to hold a dance in April from 7-11 p.m. and it proved a great success. At the April meeting, members were given a talk on Savings Certificates by a Post Office representative and agreed to form a war savings group. It was announced in May that the Missions to Seamen had received a parcel of woollies from the institute and had written to say how grateful they were. A letter from the National Federation of Women's Institutes was read at the June meeting, asking each institute to give two shillings to buy and equip an ambulance to be known as the WI's Ambulance. This ambulance was presented to the Army that same year. Yorkshire County WI headquarters asked for a register of volunteers willing to help the farmers. There was also an appeal for help at the hospital on Tuesdays, Thursdays and Fridays with mending. Thirty members

Romanby Women's Institute.

agreed to go. In July, members were busy helping with WI market stalls on the 17th and 24th. The garden meeting was still held in August at Mrs Todd's house with all funds going for our various appeals. Northallerton and District Spitfire Fund wrote to the institute in October asking for our support. The drama and choral groups offered to have an 'effort' for this fund. The annual meeting was held this year and the Christmas party was arranged for 1941.

In January, members decided to hold an open meeting about the incendiary bomb and Mr Brewer gave this in February to a large audience. In March it was reported that the Ministry of Food wished their food permit to be returned. This meant that in future, members would have to bring their own tea and sugar. There was also a letter from Mr Barraclough of the Rutson Hospital asking for the use of the WI Hall in case of emergencies and this was granted. It was also reported that fifty-four members had joined the War Savings group. The total collection in the past year was £220 12s 6d. In April arrangements were made to hold an open meeting to discuss a fruit preservation scheme and to invite Romanby residents. In May we agreed to have a jam-making centre at Romanby, starting in July. The amount invested in June for War Weapons Week was £106 10s 0d. A letter was received from the Ministry of Labour and National Service giving particulars of vacancies in work of national importance. A collection was taken in July for the bombed areas and £1 7s 0d was given. By August we knew that the jam-making session was a success and all the jam had been sold. North Mowbray Group of Women's Institutes decided to adopt the South Kensington tube centre, so Miss Blunt wrote asking Romanby WI to provide toys for the children using it, and this was done.

Around this time 500 Dixie hand-sealers or home-canners arrived from America with a complete large-scale fruit preservation unit. There were oil stoves, preserving pans, bottling jars, jam jars, jam pot covers, tea towels, thermometers and special discs for pickles and chutney. Allocations of sugar were provided by the Ministry of Food and strictly accounted for. All recipes had to be approved by the National Federation of Women's Institutes. Spot checks were frequently made. Between 1940 and 1945 more than 5,300 tons of fruit were preserved by the WI. If the fruit was available, WI members were very often expected to pick, jam and can on the spot. All work done by members and non-members was done free and all produce sold back to the ministry. Once rationing began, no member was allowed to buy from her own institute centre. Romanby WI continued to work for the war effort during 1941, helping at a communal centre kitchen, entertaining the forces, knitting, jamming and having money-making efforts to be able to help with cash where it was needed. In February, Dr McKenzie gave a talk about his experiences at the Western Front and in March, members attended a service at the Lyric Cinema in connection with Warships Week. In September of that year, Romanby WI learned that children attending Northallerton schools were not being supplied with milk, and advised York. The Milk Marketing Board started supplying the schools in October. A whist drive was held in November and all proceeds went towards Christmas gifts for local members of His Majesty's Forces serving overseas.

During 1942 a whist drive was held in aid of the British Sailors' Society. By May the target figure of £100 for War Savings 'Wings For Victory' had been passed. The total subscribed was £196 10s 0d. There was a bridge drive in aid of the National Institute for the Blind. Christmas gifts would again be supplied for HM Forces serving overseas. Instead of a Christmas party this year, Romanby WI would entertain the wounded from the RAF hospital. Fifty patients and staff attended. From March 1943 to March 1944, 739 patients from the RAF hospital were entertained to tea on Sunday afternoons. Tea was served at the bowling club for all forces personnel.

The Institute received a certificate of honour for Wings For Victory Week. Its total War Savings were £737 9s 6d. A donation of £2 was given to the Nursing Association in January 1945 and a whist drive was held for them in April, which raised £5 10s 0d. Once again the institute entertained fifty patients and staff from the hospital at Christmas. Institute members decided to hold a party once a month for the RAF hospital patients. Members were to knit cap comforts for the troops on the continent at the request of the WVS organizer. March saw members bringing gifts to be sent to people in French villages. Donations were also made to the National Institute for the Blind, the Lifeboat Institution, and the Hospital for Sick Children. A letter of thanks was received for the parcels which had been sent to France. In April we received a parcel from Brownsburg, Quebec, containing toffee, chocolate, a pound of tea and a pound of sugar. A letter of thanks was sent to Canada, which included a colour photograph of Romanby WI Hall. Romanby continued for many months to support the British Sailors' Society and Czechoslovak Friendship League.

Home and Country magazine was very much to the point when stating that there was no better time to put Women's Institutes intentions into practice than wartime. Their intentions were to make life more worthwhile for themselves and for others. Speaking at the 1943 Annual General Meeting of all Women's Institutes, Her Majesty the Queen said, 'When we have won through to peace, a great page in the history of Britain's war effort should be devoted to the country women in this dear land of ours'.

Adopting a more official pose, a Government White Paper at the end of the war stated that the high degree of mobilization in this war has been largely due to the contribution made by women.

Elsie Taylor
(Romanby WI)

Northallerton history – a wartime episode

I suppose this is a tale, albeit historical, of how South Parade lost its most notable tree.

In 1939, as in the early years of the First World War, civil defence was known as ARP – Air Raid Precautions – and was taken seriously in Northallerton. Fortunately, the county council had appointed a most efficient ARP officer, who promptly set up an organization to look after Northallerton and the rural area it served. The basement of the town hall was the control centre, with deal tables in a horseshoe layout and places for each of the Services with telephones.

The ARP controller responsible for deciding which services should be sent to any incident had the centre table. Advice of incidents would come to him by telephone, usually from the ARP wardens. Although they were better known for ensuring that no lights were showing during the blackout, they were in the front line when bombs were dropping. To ensure that an ARP controller was always available, three were appointed. They were Mr Wavell Pointing, the manager of Barclays Bank; Mr Freddie Woodhead, the Conservative party agent; and, until joining the RAF, me – then the resident inspector for the Royal Exchange Assurance, which years before had taken over the North Yorkshire Agricultural Fire Insurance Company.

Warnings of the approach of enemy aircraft were received by telephone. First came the yellow warning, when ARP key men were

The Applegarth in 1939-40.

alerted. Then came the purple warning if enemy aircraft were heading in our direction. Finally the red warning was issued when bombing was likely. All the Services were standing by on the purple warning.

There were many early warnings, as the Germans regarded Teeside and Tyneside as prime targets. Many hours were spent by the key ARP and Services personnel in readiness for action. The control centre representative of each Service would pass on the different colour warnings to his or her Service at their depots or assembly points and only on one occasion was a mistake made. Alas, the All Clear was not passed on to the rural first aid team and if any of the ladies who spent the whole of the next day on stand-by read this, perhaps it is not to late to say 'sorry'. Their representative at the time did not reveal what had happened when he passed on the purple the next evening.

The personnel in the control centre were not eligible for armed service due to their age or reserved occupations. Tribute is due to two young men in their early teens, Christopher Hird, whose father had the pharmacy in the High Street, and Harold Ankers, the ironmonger's son. Both proved to be great assets to the team.

For some time, the nearest incident was on the Osmotherley Moors, where German bombs had ignited the peat, which burned for days. Lord Haw-Haw, the English traitor who broadcast bad news from Germany, claimed hourly that Teeside was still in flames! On another occasion, the chief of the fire brigade, which in those days was manned by volunteers (the chief was a garage owner in the town), came to the town hall basement red in the face and quivering with excitement and insisting on speaking to me in private. This was only possible in the boiler room, where we huddled together in the heat. He had heard from 'higher up' in his Service that the Germans had landed in England. Fortunately, as ARP controller with access to more reliable information, I was able to reassure him.

But we did expect that sooner or later Northallerton would be targeted by German aircraft. Here was a junction of important railways, and rails can be so obvious to an airman, even at night. Likewise, Northallerton was in the centre of a network of main roads. There was also the county hall, vital to the administration of a large area that also included airfields and a military camp. In the ARP we ensured that there was every possible precaution against firebombs, although there, reliance had to be placed on 'stirrup' pumps, which were very portable but had only limited capacity.

So, one night, a German raider did straddle Northallerton with a stick of high explosive bombs. In the control room, my immediate worry was something that had caused me some private concern for a long time. In the basement there were pillars supporting the weight of the whole structure above. These appeared to be hollow cast iron. Would they shatter easily if high explosive bombs were dropped? Fortunately, although we heard the detonations, none were close enough to put the pillars to the test – but they did quiver! Messages then came in spasmodically. Some were not as quick as we hoped. There was the possibility of ARP wardens having become casualties, so I sent out our one mobile officer to explore the situation. He was Stanley Thompson. During the war he had lost his father, Walter, and found himself in charge of a small country building company with an overdraft at the bank and instructions to provide for his mother and sister. How this courageous man, who earlier had lost a leg following a motorcycle accident, converted this business into one of the largest and most successful in the county is another story. It was

typical of the man that his search for the bomb damage and succinct reports were quick and thorough. He came across one bomb crater where the water main had burst and a fountain of precious water was being hurled skywards. A warden, albeit in a state of shock, was hopefully throwing handfuls of earth at the ruptured pipe. Stanley asked us to inform the water engineers, but added, 'tell them there's no hurry. I've brayed the pipe and it's closed now'.

Other messages were coming through, and unasked, I sent first aid teams to sites where we thought casualties could have occurred. Alas, they could not save the one fatality, a serviceman. Fortunately, it being night time and the sirens having warned them, most people had taken cover, some in little Anderson shelters assembled in their gardens. One family survived in an Anderson despite an almost direct hit. The crater extended to the edge of their shelter and had scattered over the area the whole of a well-tended garden. It was behind a row of terraced houses and when I visited the site in the early morning, the tenant was standing morosely in the bottom of the crater. His neighbour was leering over the remains of the garden and I heard him say, 'What are you going to plant in there, eh?' It was an unkind remark.

There was part of a garage roof in Thirsk Road. It took some time to discover where it had come from. It had been blown over the roofs from Hatfield Road. One call after the raid was from Freddie Woodhead, complaining plaintively that his monkey-puzzle tree in his front garden in South Parade had been shattered by the blast of a bomb. I still miss it!

One fact can be recorded for history. Although many of us in the ARP might have been classed as a bunch of amateurs and in Northallerton we had not been battle-hardened, the ARP – especially the wardens out in the open and the rescue services which

Market day in the early 1940s. Sam Turner's 'stall' is outside the Golden Lion.

the controller called upon – all acted with great efficiency when the time came for action. History has also neglected another branch of our civil defence. I came across this when in the RAF and stationed temporarily in Northumberland. Rather than have Christmas dinner alone, I had as my companion (much to the annoyance of some Army officers also in the Turk's Head in Newcastle) a very bedraggled corporal of the Auxiliary Air Force. ('Really, old boy! Dining in public with an NCO – simply not done!').

The Auxiliary Air Force was manned by mostly older men who had volunteered for service prior to the outbreak of hostilities and had part-time training. They were charged with the responsibility of flying barrage balloons in target areas. My corporal was bedraggled because he was flying a balloon from a drifter anchored in the mouth of the Tyne. The quarters were cramped, the weather atrocious, the sea heaving and uniforms under inadequate capes were most of the time sodden. He had endured the blitz in London. Asked why he had been transferred north to such an appalling post, he reckoned it was some kind of punishment for having allowed his unit's mascot, a goat, to eat part of his balloon when grounded.

R.C. Dales

Memories of an evacuee

Just prior to the outbreak of the Second World War, the then manager of Sunderland Tramways decreed that all the town's tramcars should display the following notice near to the entrance and in full view of the travelling public:

'Passengers are respectfully requested to move to the front of the tramcar to allow the available accommodation to be occupied to the best advantage.'

Up until then, the conductor shouted, 'Move along, please!' and that had sufficed.

It was in a convoy of such vehicles that on 10 September 1939, a motley crowd of schoolboys was transported on the first stage of their journey, equipped and under orders, to invade the quiet market town of Northallerton.

Four hundred boys and the staff of Bede Collegiate Boys' School, clutching cases, gas masks and packets of sandwiches, were trammed to the railway station in Sunderland town centre. They were counted and recounted before being entrained for the fifty-mile journey into the 'unknown'.

We were evacuees.

As a fourteen-year-old, I recall as if it were yesterday the strange feeling of unreality at what was happening. I suppose, in a way, it was rather like men being called up for military service. Home was behind us and future surroundings and activities were unknown quantities. Anyway, after some two hours of singing and sandwich munching, the train chugged into Northallerton station and we disembarked.

I was in a large group that was guided to a hall in Romanby. There we partook of sandwiches and cups of very sweet tea provided by a band of caring ladies from the town. We were then introduced to our foster parents and dispersed in small groups to our new temporary homes. Many of the boys had never been away from their families and homesickness was already being felt.

I was more fortunate than most of the boys. The person I was 'assigned' to was a friend of my mother. She was Mrs Rene Drinkald of

Bede Collegiate School, Sunderland, 1938.

Bede Boys' Collegiate School football team, 1939. They were evacuated to Northallerton on 10 September 1939.

The whole school after arrival in Northallerton. One of the pupils, Peter Kirby, took this picture. In the background is Northallerton Grammar School, which was shared with the evacuees.

No. 56 Crosby Road. She and my mother had worked together in Sunderland before either of them was married and had kept up the friendship over the twenty years before the war started. Indeed, my family had spent several holidays at her home. So for me, it was neither meeting new people nor entering a strange house.

When I arrived, I found to my amazement that Mrs Drinkald's nephew was the second evacuee. He was known to me at school but I had had no knowledge of his relationship with our foster mother. We were ushered upstairs to our bedroom and, sitting on the edge of the bed, we wrote postcards to our parents back in Sunderland, confirming our safe arrival.

The rural atmosphere of Northallerton and the friendliness of all the people impressed me greatly. We shared the grammar school with the local pupils. Usually, they attended school in the mornings while we 'outsiders' were on the afternoon shift from 1 to 5 p.m. The arrangement worked very well and we soon settled down to our education in new surroundings and made light of any difficulties. The teaching staff of both schools did a magnificent job, doing everything in their power to normalize a situation that was very far from the norm.

The vast majority of the hosts and hostesses were unstinting in their efforts to make the boys comfortable. Of course, a few incompatibilities were bound to arise. For example, my cousin was billeted with a couple who just didn't understand boys. He was fed nothing but ham and tomatoes at every meal for a fortnight. He was very unhappy. However, the problem eventually righted itself and, like all the rest of us, he settled down to the new life.

Northallerton, like all towns, changed considerably as soon as war was declared. Lots of military training was carried out in the area and uniforms abounded. I believe the prison was militarized and army dispatch riders could

No. 56 Crosby Road as it is today.

Northallerton Grammar School in 1939.

be seen every day, training on their BSA motorcycles on the nearby field at the bottom of Crosby Road. The new fighters of the RAF from Catterick could be seen daily. We boys eagerly plane-spotted the new Hurricanes and Spitfires as they prepared to defend the skies over northern England.

We evacuees were there because it was expected that Sunderland, being a highly industrialized area and the largest shipbuilding town in the world, would be bombed by the *Luftwaffe* in the very early stages of the war. Strangely, that did not happen. Indeed, the first signs of enemy aerial activity occurred

South Parade in the 1930s.

over the very place we had been sent to for safety. The siren sounded a number of times early in 1940, and we spent sleepless nights in the cupboard under the stairs at No. 56. A bomb dropped on the fields at the end of Crosby Road and we boys were up the following morning collecting shrapnel to show to our pals at school. Bombs fell too along South Parade. A number of schoolboys returned to Sunderland, preferring to share the dangers with their families rather than with strangers.

Now, more than sixty years on, I just have to think about evacuation and vignettes flash into my mind of incidences, situations and involvements I experienced from the early days of September, 1939 to the summer of 1940 when I returned home to complete my education in more familiar surroundings – before I too became a member of the armed forces. I enjoyed every minute I spent in the rural atmosphere of Northallerton. I cannot praise too highly the efforts of the local population for their contribution to the war effort by welcoming so many strangers into their homes. I have visited the town a number

of times in later life and have relived my days there as I walked the streets and yards. I remember the exciting travelling fair that coincided with our arrival in the town. It was sited near to the Anglican church and gave great pleasure during the late summer evenings.

I still have nightmares of that Sunday evening when my friend and I contrived between us to drop the full collection plate in the gallery of the Methodist church. The coins seemed to bounce down the wooden stairs forever! And how well I remember the old cinema on the main street and the fish and chip shop that sold peas sprinkled among the chips.

One evening up a side yard, I witnessed the slaughter of a huge pig by two of the local butchers. The sight and sounds haunted me for years.

Blackberry picking, cycle rides through the nearby villages, scouting activities, my very first girlfriend, Jeanne Cowans, and the many activities I pursued as a teenager – all these make up the boulders of my memory dam that will never be destroyed by the passage of time.

Wilson Taylor